This is my favourite...

THE BBC CHILDREN IN NEED RECIPE BOOK 2005

"THIS IS MY FAVOURITE" IS MADE UP OF 100 ORIGINAL RECIPES FROM SOME OF THE COUNTRY'S BEST KNOWN CHEFS; GORDON RAMSAY, GARY RHODES, RAYMOND BLANC, MICHEL ROUX, HESTON BLUMENTHAL, ANTONY WORRALL THOMPSON. ADD TO THESE A LIST OF CHEFS WHO MAY NOT BE AS WELL KNOWN, BUT WHO ARE JUST AS PASSIONATE ABOUT THE RECIPES THEY CREATE. THEY ALL HAVE ONE THING IN COMMON, THE DESIRE TO PRODUCE GREAT TASTING FOOD.

WITH THANKS

IT'S ONLY WHEN YOU COME TO THE END OF A PROJECT AND YOU HAVE THE OPPORTUNITY TO LOOK BACK, THAT YOU RECOGNISE THE ENORMOUS EFFORTS THAT HAVE BEEN MADE BY EVERYONE CONCERNED. THAT HAS CERTAINLY BEEN THE CASE IN TAKING THIS BOOK TO PUBLICATION. SO, IN NO PARTICULAR ORDER, A BIG 'THANK YOU' TO THE PEOPLE WHO MADE 'THIS IS MY FAVOURITE' NOT ONLY A POSSIBILITY BUT A REALITY.

FIRSTLY, TO JONATHAN FORD AND ZAHRA CLARK; THEIR PASSION AND ENTHUSIASM TO DELIVER THIS PROJECT AT TIMES HAS DRIVEN US ALL TO QUESTION BOTH THEIR SANITY AND OURS! MY CREATIVE DIRECTOR, ANDY SHARP, AND ALL OF HIS DESIGN AND PRODUCTION TEAM; KAREN KAVDE, DARREN JACKSON, MATT JETTEN, SIMON MARSHALL, SIMON TUCKER, KATE GRIFFITHS, RUSSELL EDMUNDSON AND PHIL COLLINS (PHOTOGRAPHY).

RACHEL FORDER AND THE DAILY TELEGRAPH, WHOSE SERIALISATION OF THE BOOK HAS HELPED RAISE AWARENESS AND INTEREST THROUGHOUT THE COUNTRY. THE MILLENNIUM HOTEL'S MJU RESTAURANT AND, IN PARTICULAR, CHEF TOM THOMSEN, JEREMY PAYNE AND HELEN TREVORROW FOR HOSTING THE LAUNCH OF 'THIS IS MY FAVOURITE'.

STEVE WINDUSS AND MAGGI FOX, WHOSE ADVICE AND GUIDANCE HAS PROVED INVALUABLE. LAURA EDWARDS, NAOMI SNUGGS AND PAULA NUTBEAM WHO HAVE ASSISTED US ALL THROUGHOUT. MY FATHER MIKE, WHOSE PROOF READING SKILLS HAVE BECOME THE SUBJECT OF LEGEND!

THE CHEFS THEMSELVES, ALL 100 OF THEM, WITHOUT WHOM 'THIS IS MY FAVOURITE' WOULD NOT HAVE BEEN POSSIBLE. AND, LAST BUT NOT LEAST, EVERYONE WHO BUYS THE BOOK AND, IN SO DOING, HELPS US TO HELP THE BBC CHILDREN IN NEED APPEAL.

THANK YOU, ENJOY THE RECIPES AND LET US KNOW WHICH IS YOUR FAVOURITE BY GOING TO: WWW.THISISMYFAVOURITE.CO.UK.

CHRIS RANSOM

THE BBC CHILDREN IN NEED APPEAL

In support of

BBC CHILDREN IN NEED

THE BBC CHILDREN IN NEED APPEAL HELPS DISADVANTAGED CHILDREN AND YOUNG PEOPLE IN THE UK. SOME HAVE EXPERIENCED DOMESTIC VIOLENCE, NEGLECT, HOMELESSNESS OR SEXUAL ABUSE, WHILE OTHERS HAVE SUFFERED FROM SERIOUS ILLNESSES, OR HAVE HAD TO LEARN TO DEAL WITH PROFOUND DISABILITIES FROM A VERY YOUNG AGE.

MANY ORGANISATIONS SUPPORTED BY THE CHARITY AIM TO CREATE A LASTING IMPACT ON CHILDREN'S LIVES. SOME OFFER LOW ACHIEVING CHILDREN FROM AREAS OF DEPRIVATION A CHANCE TO DEVELOP THEIR EDUCATIONAL SKILLS AND AMBITIONS, AND OTHERS CREATE OPPORTUNITIES FOR YOUNG PEOPLE WHO ARE HOMELESS OR SOCIALLY EXCLUDED, TO ENABLE THEM TO MOVE FORWARD AND SECURE A FULFILLING FUTURE. THE CHARITY OFFERS GRANTS TO VOLUNTARY AND COMMUNITY GROUPS AND REGISTERED CHARITIES AROUND THE UK THAT FOCUS ON IMPROVING CHILDREN'S LIVES. GRANTS ARE TARGETED ON THE AREAS OF GREATEST NEED, AND MONEY IS ALLOCATED GEOGRAPHICALLY TO ENSURE THAT CHILDREN IN ALL CORNERS OF THE UK HAVE A FAIR SHARE OF THE MONEY RAISED.

FOR MORE INFORMATION EMAIL: PUDSEY@BBC.CO.UK OR TELEPHONE: 020 8576 7788. YOU CAN ALSO VISIT OUR WEBSITE AT: BBC.CO.UK/PUDSEY.

PUBLISHED BY THE RANSOM GROUP

© THE RANSOM GROUP 2005

BBC CHILDREN IN NEED APPEAL COMMERCIAL PARTICIPATION NUMBER CMC/05/10

PRINTED IN GREAT BRITAIN BY BUTLER AND TANNER LTD.

ISBN 0-9551331-0-6

'THIS IS MY FAVOURITE'
WESTWOOD CENTRE
NUTWOOD WAY
SOUTHAMPTON SO40 3SZ
INFO@THISISMYFAVOURITE.CO.UK
WWW.THISISMYFAVOURITE.CO.UK

BBC CHILDREN IN NEED APPEAL IS A REGISTERED CHARITY, NO.802052

CONTENTS

This is my favourite...

THE BBC CHILDREN IN NEED RECIPE BOOK 2005

ALLIUM TART - ROASTED SHALLOTS WITH GLAZED GOAT'S CHEESE

INGREDIENTS:

2 Crottin de Chavignol
(or a similar form of goat's cheese)
200ml olive oil
3 garlic cloves
1 sprig of thyme
1 sprig of rosemary
200g puff pastry
1kg shallots, peeled
400ml chicken stock
Basil oil (1 litre olive oil, 1kg basil)
50ml balsamic vinegar
Salt & black pepper mill

METHOD:

Cut the cheese in half and place in the olive oil with the garlic, rosemary and thyme. Marinate for at least four hours or overnight for extra flavour. Remove and dry.

Heat a little of the oil from the cheese in a double-bottomed pan and place the shallots inside. The shallots should just cover the bottom of the pan, there should not be any free space, neither should they be on top of each other. Fry until coloured on all sides and pour away the oil, then add the chicken stock. Simmer on the stove until the jus has reduced, then cover and place in the oven. Braise until they are cooked well at 160°C, for approximately 45 minutes. Remove and divide the shallots into 10cm wide non-stick moulds.

Roll out the puff pastry until approximately 1/2cm thick and cut out 10cm discs. Place on top of the shallots and bake in the oven at 200°C, until puff pastry is golden brown, approximately 20 minutes. Turn out on a plate.

Grill the goat's cheese until slightly brown and hot. Place on top of the tart. Drizzle a little basil oil and the balsamic vinegar around the dish.

TO MAKE THE BASIL OIL
Pick basil leaves from stalks, blanch and refresh in iced water. Squeeze dry, place all ingredients in food blender - blitz for 25 minutes. Push through chinois, making sure you get every drop out. Allow to drain through two coffee filters, and store in kilner jars.

Anton Edelmann
Chef Patron

CHEF SAYS...

ANTON EDELMANN IS THE CHEF PATRON FOR THE ALLIUM, LONDON

" Our Allium Tart is the ultimate in depths of flavour of shallots, melted goat's cheese and herb salad; and now is a classic! "

Anton Edelmann

CHEF SAYS...

STEVEN PIDGEON IS THE HEAD CHEF FOR THE ARUNDELL ARMS

" This is a recipe which is quick and easy to prepare and it is a change from the usual roasted pheasant. The sage and pancetta really complement the pheasant. "

Steven Pidgeon

SAGE ROASTED PHEASANT WITH SAVOY CABBAGE AND CRISPY PANCETTA

SERVES: 4
PREPARATION TIME: 20 MINUTES
COOKING TIME: 30-45 MINUTES

INGREDIENTS:
140g butter
2 young pheasants
Salt and pepper
4 sprigs sage
500ml dry cider
290ml double cream
8 slices pancetta
8 tablespoons olive oil
1 Savoy cabbage

METHOD:
Heat the olive oil and butter in a roasting tin and season the pheasants with salt, pepper and sage. Place in the roasting tray in a preheated oven at 190°C/375°F/Gas Mark 5. Keep turning and basting the pheasants every 5-7 minutes. Keep in the oven for about 30 minutes. Once the pheasants are cooked, place them on a chopping board. Remove the legs and breasts and set aside. Keep warm.

Chop each carcass into four pieces and place back into the roasting tray with the cider. Simmer for 5 minutes. Remove carcasses from roasting tray. Strain the sauce into a pan and reduce by half, then add the cream and simmer for 5 minutes or until the sauce is slightly thickened.

Place the pheasant joints back into the roasting tray to warm through. Then cut the Savoy cabbage into four and remove the core, chop finely and sweat off in a little butter (85g) and season.

Pan fry the pancetta in a little olive oil. Place the cabbage on a dish, put the pheasant joints on top and cover with sauce. Garnish with the fried pancetta.

S Pidgeon

Steven Pidgeon
Head Chef

13

LANCASHIRE CAESAR SALAD

SERVES: 4

INGREDIENTS:
1 small baguette
3 garlic cloves
4 tablespoons extra virgin olive oil
2 anchovy fillets
1 pot sour cream (142ml)
Juice and zest of half a lemon
2 romaine or cos lettuces
2 little gem lettuces
1 bunch of freshly chopped flat parsley
150g crumbled Lancashire cheese
Sea salt and freshly ground pepper

METHOD:
Pre-heat an oven to 200°C/400°F/Gas Mark 5. Make croutons by cutting baguette into large chunks, drizzle with 2 tablespoons of olive oil and rub with 2 cloves of garlic, bake for 6-8 minutes.

Make the dressing, in a blender or liquidizer add the sour cream, 1 clove garlic, anchovies, lemon juice and zest, and the remaining olive oil. Blend until smooth, remove from blender then stir in 100g of crumbled Lancashire cheese, if this is a little thick add some milk to loosen to a dressing consistency, season with salt and pepper.

Pour the dressing in a large bowl, add the salad leaves, croutons, chopped parsley and the remaining cheese, tumble the dressing over leaves and croutons then serve.

Neil Nugent
Asda Brand Chef

CHEF SAYS...
NEIL NUGENT IS ASDA BRAND CHEF

" This Caesar recipe uses one of my favourite cheeses from my homeland - Lancashire, it also works well with a poached egg on top. "

Neil Nugent

14

BRUNELLO AT THE BAGLIONI HOTEL, LONDON

Hyde Park Gate, Kensington, London, SW7 5BB. Telephone: 020 7368 5700

CHEF SAYS...

STEFANO STECCA IS THE HEAD CHEF FOR BAGLIONI

" Let the meat dry in the fridge for two days and then apply fruit mustard to it before covering it in breadcrumbs. "

Stefano Stecca

VEAL CHOP MILANESE

INGREDIENTS:
200g veal strip loin cut in 2 cubes
100g breadcrumbs
1 egg
Flour
Cleared butter
150g lettuce
30g fruit mustard
Veal sauce
Cherry tomatoes

METHOD:
Clean the strip loins and cut in 2 cubes. Soak into the eggs and then in flour and then again into the eggs. Lay the cubes into breadcrumbs. Cook the Milan cubes in clear butter. Pan-fry the lettuce in olive oil, on the side. Drain the lettuce and place in the middle of the plate. Place a cube on top of the lettuce and the other cube must be cut and placed on the side. Blend the fruit mustard and decorate the plate with 2 lines of the blended mustard.

Stefano Stecca
Head Chef

BANK RESTAURANTS

Aldwych, Birmingham & Westminster, 15-19 Kingsway, London, WC2B 6UN. Telephone: 020 7379 9797 Online: www.bankrestaurants.com

CHICKEN SUPREME GRATIN

SERVES: 4

INGREDIENTS:
4 supreme chicken
80g chicken jus
300g wild mushrooms
10g butter
2 egg yolks for sabayon
5ml olive oil
50ml water
Salt and pepper
50ml white wine

METHOD:
Cook the chicken in a frying pan with the butter and olive oil for approximately 10 minutes - put to one side.

Sauté the wild mushrooms in a frying pan, season to taste. When the mushrooms are cooked, drain away all of the mushroom juice. Using a different frying pan, sauté the mushrooms again until they are golden brown - put to one side. If you like parsley or garlic, or both, add them to the mushrooms. Make the sabayon by slowly whisking egg yolks with the white wine and water. Slowly whisk the mixture over a low heat until the consistency thickens.

Place the mushrooms in the middle of the plate. Slice the chicken supreme into fine slices. Place each slice over the mushrooms until they are all covered. Pour the sabayon over the mushrooms and chicken and glaze under the grill.

Christian Delteil
Managing Director

Christian Delteil

CHEF SAYS...

CHRISTIAN DELTEIL IS MANAGING DIRECTOR FOR BANK RESTAURANTS

" It is great when we can use our Chef skills to support worthy charities such as BBC Children in Need. "

16

CHEF SAYS...

BERNHARD ENGELHARDT IS RESEARCH DEVELOPMENT CHEF

" This dessert combines the flavours of classic German Christmas Cake and traditional English Bread and Butter Pudding giving a surprising, but very tasty treat. "

Bernhard Engelhardt

STOLLEN BREAD & BUTTER PUDDING WITH KIRSCH MARINATED CHERRIES

SERVES: 4

INGREDIENTS:

BREAD & BUTTER PUDDING
240g diced brioche
20g chopped mixed peel
40g marzipan
8g currants
8g raisins
2g mixed spice
300ml double cream
4 whole eggs
20g caster sugar

WHITE CHOCOLATE SAUCE
60g white chocolate
100ml double cream

MARINATED CHERRIES
120g black cherries
16ml Kirsch
5g corn flour

GARNISH
10g icing sugar
20g demerara sugar for glaze
4 mint tip

VANILLA BEAN ICE CREAM
4 x 30g (you can buy this in the shop)

METHOD:

Make an egg custard with the sugar, double cream, whole egg and mixed spice. Layer diced brioche, raisins, currants and flaked marzipan in pudding moulds and fill with egg custard. Allow to stand for 10 minutes, refill if necessary.

Place in 120°C oven for 30 minutes or until set and light golden brown. Rest pudding in the mould for about 10 minutes before turning out. Sprinkle demerara sugar on the turned out pudding and glaze under a grill or with a blowtorch.

Heat double cream, remove from heat and stir in white chocolate until melted. Drain the black cherries and bring the juice to the boil. Thicken the boiling juice up with a corn flour mix. Add the Kirsch Liquor.

Dust the pudding with a little icing sugar, place on the serving plate, arrange the cherries around the pudding and drizzle with the white chocolate sauce. Serve warm with good quality ice cream and a refreshing mint sprig, and enjoy.

Bernhard Engelhardt
Research Development Chef

17

BERKELEY SQUARE RESTAURANT, LONDON

No 7 Davis Street, Mayfair, London, W1K 3DD. Telephone: 020 7629 6993

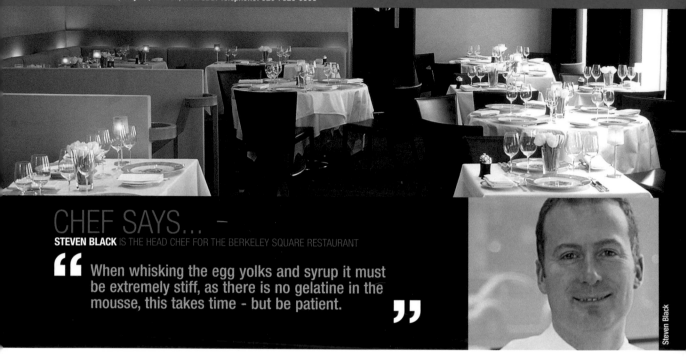

CHEF SAYS...

STEVEN BLACK IS THE HEAD CHEF FOR THE BERKELEY SQUARE RESTAURANT

" When whisking the egg yolks and syrup it must be extremely stiff, as there is no gelatine in the mousse, this takes time - but be patient. "

Steven Black

CHAMPAGNE MOUSSE WITH RASPBERRY SABLE AND RASPBERRY SORBET

SERVES: 6

INGREDIENTS:

CHAMPAGNE MOUSSE
50g champagne
15g caster sugar
2 egg yolks
Drop of water
1 egg white
25g champagne
1 leaf of gelatine
50g double cream
65g champagne
SABLE BISCUIT
140g icing sugar
340g soft unsalted butter
Zest of 1 lemon
45g egg whites
450g plain flour
RASPBERRY SORBET
500g raspberry purée
½ litre water
150g sugar
Juice from ¼ lemon
FOR PLATING
2 punnets of raspberries
Fresh mint
Raspberry sauce

METHOD:

CHAMPAGNE MOUSSE

Make a syrup with 50g champagne and 15g sugar, keep warm. Put egg yolks on a bain-marie (pan of steaming water with a bowl that fits in it) start to whisk vigorously. Pour syrup in gently while whisking until it becomes zabaglione (stiff foam).

Bring 30g sugar and a drop of water to 121°C. Start to whisk egg whites when the sugar is at 118°C. When the sugar is at 121°C pour into the stiff egg whites (keep whisking at slow beat) and allow to cool.

Warm 65g of champagne and add soaked gelatine, stir until dissolved, this is for the jelly. Whip double cream until stiff, fold in zabaglione and egg whites, add 25g champagne and pour into square moulds (4cm square, by 2cm deep). Do not fill to the top, leave to set in the fridge. Pour on jelly and re-set.

SABLE BISCUIT

In a mixer add icing sugar and soft butter and mix until even. Add zest and egg whites and mix till smooth. Add flour and mix until it looks like pastry, then take out and put in cling film, leave in fridge for 2 hours to rest.

Roll out and cut into large round discs (7.5cm diameter) and bake on silicone paper for 5-10 minutes at 180°C.

RASPBERRY SORBET

Add all ingredients together and bring to the boil, then leave to cool. Churn in an ice cream machine and freeze.

Steven Black
Head Chef

ROASTED COD WITH BUTTERBEAN AND CHORIZO STEW

INGREDIENTS:
4 nice thick cod pieces 175g in weight each
100ml olive oil
400g butterbeans
400g tinned chopped tomatoes
300g cooking chorizo, sliced
200ml white wine
1 tablespoon tomato paste
5 garlic gloves, finely chopped
1 large onion, diced
4 rosemary sprigs, chopped
2 teaspoons smoked paprika
1 tablespoon of sugar
A good handful of flat parsley, finely chopped

METHOD:
Soak beans in lots of water for 8 hours. Then drain off the water and place beans in a large pan with about 3 pints of salted water and cook until soft. Then refresh the beans under cold water.

Whilst the beans are cooking heat a pan with the olive oil and add the onions and garlic. Cook until they are soft and sweet to taste. Add the tomato paste and red wine then cook for about a minute.

Mix in the cooked beans, chorizo, rosemary and paprika and then add the sugar to balance the acidity. Season with salt and pepper then cover with foil. Cook in a preheated oven (200°C/400°F/Gas Mark 6) for about an hour. When the cooking time is up take it out of the oven and leave it covered on top of the stove.

Brush the cod with a little olive oil, salt and pepper and cook for about 10-15 minutes (depending on the size of the fish). Uncover the beans and finish with lots of freshly chopped parsley and then it is ready to serve.

Adrian Geddes
Head Chef

Adrian Geddes

CHEF SAYS:...
ADRIAN GEDDES IS HEAD CHEF FOR THE BLANCH HOUSE RESTAURANT

" Make sure you do not overcook the fish. Serve the dish with some good bread. This is a really easy dish to do at home. The stew can be made in advance to use later. "

BOURNEMOUTH SCHOOL OF CATERING

The Lansdowne, Bournemouth, BH1 3JJ. Telephone: 01202 205831 Fax: 01202 205980 Online: www.thecollege.co.uk

CHEF SAYS...

TONY GROVES IS SENIOR LECTURER IN FOOD PREPARATION

" Cookery should be fun, full of enjoyment and self expression - not a chore. I have cooked professionally for 35 years yet still learn something different about food every single day. "

Tony Groves

SMOKED CHICKEN, AVOCADO, MIXED LEAF SALAD AND WALNUT DRESSING

SERVES: 2

INGREDIENTS:
1 smoked chicken breast
(available at most delis or supermarkets)
1 ripe avocado pear
1 blanched and skinned tomato
2 chives
Mixed lettuce leaves - curly endive,
lollo rosso, corn salad
DRESSING
3 tablespoons walnut oil
1 tablespoon white wine vinegar
Grain mustard to taste
Salt and pepper
DECORATION
Reduced balsamic vinegar
Smoked paprika

METHOD:
Peel the avocado and divide in half, remove the stone. Slice the avocado and dress neatly on the plate, season with salt and pepper mill and spoon with a little dressing.

Slice the smoked chicken breast and brush with walnut oil. Arrange neatly covering two thirds of the avocado.

Spoon a few drops of the reduced balsamic syrup around the edge of the plate and feather with a cocktail stick. Arrange picked and washed salad leaves onto the chicken and avocado, dress with the walnut dressing, this will help the salad adhere to the food and improve the taste.

Finally sprinkle with a little smoked paprika to enhance the flavours and appearance.

Tony Groves
Senior Lecturer in Food Preparation

BUCKINGHAM PALACE

London, SW1A 1AA

CHEF SAYS...

MARK FLANAGAN ROYAL CHEF

" This is one of my favourite dishes as it is a light summery recipe combining the flavours of saffron and orange to give a refreshing clean taste complementing a delicious native fish. "

Mark Flanagan
© Royal Collection

FILLET OF HALIBUT ESCABECHE

INGREDIENTS:

250g onions
4 sticks celery
1 bulb of fennel
200g carrots
1 large sprig of thyme
1 clove of garlic
1 bayleaf
10 white peppercorns
Coarse sea salt
15g coriander seeds
Good pinch of saffron
75ml white wine vinegar
250ml white wine
250ml fresh orange juice
175ml extra virgin olive oil
4 x 150g each fresh halibut portions
1/4 bunch fresh coriander

METHOD:

Prepare the vegetables by slicing the onions thinly, de-string the fennel and cut into segment-like wedges, peel and de-string the celery and cut thin slices on the angle, canele (channel) the carrots and cut into thin rounds.

Combine all the liquids in a large casserole pan, put the herbs and spices in a little muslin bag and allow to infuse in the liquid on a medium heat for 3-4 minutes, when the liquid comes to the boil add the carrots and onions, simmer for 2 minutes and then add the fennel and celery. Cook gently and remove from the stove just before the vegetables are cooked then add the fillets of halibut, cover with foil and bake in a medium hot oven for approximately 4 minutes, turn the fish over and cook for a further 2 minutes or until the fish is just cooked.

Remove the fish and vegetables from the pan and keep warm. Pass the sauce through a strainer into another pan, and reduce the liquid rapidly, tasting continually until you reach the desired consistency, adjust the seasoning if necessary.

Arrange the fish and vegetables onto a serving dish and pour the sauce over, then add a little chopped coriander leaf (optional).

Mark Flanagan
Royal Chef

EUREST BRITISH AIRWAYS

British Airways Waterside, PO Box 365, Harmondsworth, UB7 0GB. Online: www.ba.com

STICKY DATE AND HAZELNUT PUDDING SERVED WITH BAILEYS ICE CREAM

SERVES: 4

INGREDIENTS:

90g dates, stoned and chopped
150ml water
1/2 teaspoon bicarbonate of soda
25g unsalted butter
90g soft dark brown sugar
1 egg, beaten
90g self raising flour
1/2 teaspoon vanilla essence
40g toasted chopped hazelnuts
BAILEYS ICE CREAM
125g caster sugar
1 1/2 fl oz water
1/2 litre milk
6 egg yolks
1/4 ltr double cream
2 tots Baileys

METHOD:

Cover the dates with the water and cook for about 5 minutes until soft. Add the bicarbonate of soda. In a mixing bowl cream the butter and the sugar until light and fluffy then add the egg. Mix in the dates then the flour and essence and fold together. Pipe into greased buttered and lined moulds and bake for approximately 15-20 minutes on 180°C/350°F/Gas Mark 4.

BAILEYS ICE CREAM

Bring the milk to the boil in a saucepan, whisk the egg yolks and caster sugar in a bowl until pale and creamy. Add the warm milk to the egg and sugar mix, then return the mixture to heat and cook out until it coats the back of the spoon, taking care not to overcook or boil the mixture.

Allow to cool. Once cooled add the Baileys. Place into the ice cream churner and churn, once well chilled add the double cream and finish until frozen.

TO ASSEMBLE THE DISH

In a warm bowl place a small amount of the sauce anglaise reserved earlier. Place a hot pudding on top of the sauce. Place a scoop of ice cream on top of the dessert. Top with a chocolate stick.

Nick Vadis
Eurest British Airways Chef

CHEF SAYS...

NICK VADIS IS THE CHEF FOR EUREST BRITISH AIRWAYS

" This dish is a superb winter dessert; it is simple to make and eats well, a favourite in the British Airways first class pre-flight dining in the lounges at Heathrow. Enjoy. "

Nick Vadis

CHEF SAYS...

MICHAEL CROFT IS EXECUTIVE HEAD CHEF DIRECTOR FOR CALCOT MANOR

" In every dish you cook, always remember to add the most important ingredient of all: love. "

Michael Croft

LANGOUSTINE TAGLIOLINI WITH BROAD BEANS, MINT & BASIL

SERVES: 6

INGREDIENTS:
35 langoustine tails - large and fresh
500g homemade tagliolini pasta
250g podded fresh broad beans
1 small chilli
1/2 clove garlic
Olive oil - the best you can get
2-3 peeled Italian shallots
3 large plum tomatoes
1 lemon
Bunches of basil, mint and coriander

METHOD:

Peel the langoustine carefully and retain the shells. Finely chop the shallots, garlic and red chilli (discarding the hot seeds first!) In a large pan of boiling water blanch the tomatoes and plunge into ice cold water, likewise the broad beans then peel both and de-seed the tomatoes and cut into a neat dice.

Crush the langoustine shells lightly and fry in oil in a large heavy bottomed pan, add the shallot trimmings and a small amount of garlic - carrot, celery and fennel can also be added, sauté for a few moments, add some tomato trimmings and a little white wine and water and simmer gently.

After 20 minutes drain the langoustine stock and reduce to an essence - it should be oily like a flavoured oil/dressing. Have your homemade tagliolini ready to cook in a large pot of boiling salted and oiled water - it should cook in 2-3 minutes only.

In a sauté pan heat a little olive oil and fry your langoustine tails for 2-3 minutes each side and remove to a plate and keep warm. Add some more oil to the pan and fry some chopped shallot, chilli and garlic, cook for 1-2 minutes then add the broad beans, tomato, coriander and mint - finally add the cooked tagliolini, mix together quickly and gently using a fork or pasta server.

Serve into bowls or a large serving platter and drizzle with the langoustine oil dressing.

Michael Croft
Executive Head Chef Director

CHESTER GROSVENOR AND SPA

The Arkle, Eastgate, Chester, Cheshire, CH1 1LT. Telephone: 01244 324024 Email: hotel@chestergrosvenor.com Online: www.chestergrosvenor.com

CHEF SAYS...

SIMON RADLEY IS THE EXECUTIVE CHEF FOR THE CHESTER GROSVENOR AND SPA

" This is a great dish where good quality ingredients really shine through. The preparation is fairly involved but persevere, it's worth it! "

Simon Radley

SCOTTISH LOBSTER AND SWEETBREADS

SERVES: 4

INGREDIENTS:
2 x 500g lobsters
4 x 275g veal sweetbreads, blanched and skinned
500g pasta flour
10 egg yolks
2 eggs
Pinch of saffron strands, steeped in hot water
MILD CURRY SPICE
10g turmeric
2g chilli powder
5g cardamom pods
5g fennel seed
5g coriander seeds
5g cumin seeds
200g blanched almonds
MIREPOIX VEGETABLES
(1 each of carrot, onion & celery stalk, diced)
500ml fish stock
500ml whipping cream
500g chickpeas
250ml chicken stock
12 x Pak Choi leaves (or spinach)
Curry oil
Olive Oil

METHOD:

Blanch the lobsters in boiling water for 4 minutes, then chill and shell. Separate the claws, split the tails in half and remove the entrails. Mix the pasta flour, saffron water, eggs, yolks and a pinch of salt. Add a splash of olive oil. Knead together, then rest for an hour before rolling out to the finest setting on a pasta machine. Cut into strips 25cm (10") long by 5cm (2") wide. Blanch and refresh.

Roast the curry spices in a dry pan, then crush and mix. Sweat the mirepoix in hot oil, then add a pinch of the curry spice. Sweat again and add the fish stock and reduce the liquid by half. Add the cream and reduce again by half then finely strain the curry cream.

Toast the almonds in foaming butter until they are golden brown, remove and sprinkle with salt. Cook the chickpeas in chicken stock until they are soft, then purée and strain, keeping back a fifth for garnish. Fry the sweetbreads in foaming butter until they are

golden and cooked through. Reheat the lobster in a butter and water emulsion.

Warm the pasta in salted water with a splash of olive oil and wrap one sheet around each sweetbread. Blanch the Pak Choi or spinach leaves and arrange on the pasta topped with half a lobster tail and a claw.

Reheat the cooked chickpeas and almonds and scatter them around the plate. Dress with curry oil and the curry cream, foamed with a hand blender. Decorate the plate with toasted cumin and coriander seeds.

Simon Radley
Executive Chef

CHEWTON GLEN, NEW MILTON

New Milton, Hampshire, BH25 6QS. Telephone: 01425 282268

CHEF SAYS...

LUKE MATTHEWS IS THE HEAD CHEF FOR THE CHEWTON GLEN

" It was a pleasure to be asked to contribute my recipe to such a worthwhile cause and I hope you enjoy it as much as I do. "

Luke Matthews

FILLET OF SCOTTISH BEEF, CEP MUSHROOMS AND POTATO FONDANT

INGREDIENTS:
4 fillet steaks
4 sticks salsify
12 baby onions
6 cep mushrooms
4 potato fondants
4 Jerusalem artichokes
300ml Madeira sauce
MADEIRA SAUCE
500gm beef trimmings (sautéed) add;
1 clove garlic
1 bay leaf
1/2 carrot
1 celery stick
1/2 medium onion
375ml Madeira, reduced by half
THEN ADD:
500ml chicken stock
500ml demi glaze, reduced by half, pass, then add 10g butter

METHOD:
FONDANT POTATO
With a round cutter cut out from Maris Piper potatoes 4 round disks. Well butter a frying pan and season. Lay potatoes in flat side down, cover with water, add another 100g of butter. Cook slowly on both sides till soft. Water should evaporate and the butter will colour the potato.

SALSIFY
Wash well and peel. Cut each stick into 3 even pieces, blanch in boiling salted water and refresh.

SPINACH
Destalk and wash. Blanch in boiling salted water, refresh.

JERUSALEM ARTICHOKE
Wash and peel. Cut into round disks and cook in a little chicken stock till tender.

CEPS
Cut in half and cook on one side in a little butter till golden brown.

Pan fry the steaks in a little vegetable oil and butter. At the same time warm through all the other components. Sauté the spinach in a little beurre noisette and finish the sauce with a little chopped truffle. Arrange on a flat white plate, add the sauce and serve.

Luke Matthews
Head Chef

28

CHOCOLATE & CARDAMOM CAKE WITH CINNAMON ICE CREAM

INGREDIENTS:

FOR THE CHOCOLATE & CARDAMOM CAKE
150g soft unsalted butter
150g soft brown sugar
110g plain flour
2 teaspoons baking powder
4 large eggs
90g bitter dark chocolate, melted in a saucepan over hot - but not boiling water
2 teaspoons cardamom powder, ground finely from 13-15 green cardamom pods
FOR THE CINNAMON ICE CREAM
7 large egg yolks
125g caster sugar
3 teaspoons very fine cinnamon powder
560ml double cream

METHOD:

CHOCOLATE AND CARDAMOM CAKE
Warm the butter until soft. Mix the sugar and butter together in a bowl until smooth (this can be done in a mixing machine or by hand). Beat in the eggs one by one. Sieve the flour and baking powder into the mixture and continue mixing slowly. Add the cardamom powder and continue mixing slowly. Fold in the chocolate and continue mixing slowly until a consistent mixture is achieved.

Line a 11cm x 19cm loaf tin with buttered greaseproof paper. Pour in the mixture and steam for 30-45 minutes in a steamer.

CINNAMON ICE CREAM
Mix the sugar and egg yolks until smooth. Mix in the cinnamon powder and double cream. Churn in an ice cream maker and freeze.

Adu Amran Hassan
Head Chef

Adu Amran Hassan

CHEF SAYS...

ADU AMRAN HASSAN IS HEAD CHEF FOR CHAMPOR-CHAMPOR

" Southeast Asian cuisine is all about balance and passion. It is not just a matter of adding coriander or lemon grass to a recipe! "

30

CHEF SAYS...

MATT OWENS IS THE EXECUTIVE PASTRY CHEF FOR CIRCADIA

" Simple flavours and textures for that perfect finish. "

Matt Owens

CHOCOLATE BROWNIE, ORANGE SORBET & A SHOT OF RASPBERRY & LEMON

SERVES: 8

INGREDIENTS:

BROWNIE
100g dark couverture
50g unsalted butter
2 whole eggs
75g caster sugar
1/4 teaspoon vanilla essence
75g soft flour
2g baking powder
50g chopped pecans

SORBET
75ml freshly squeezed orange juice
75ml water
50g sugar
5g cocoa powder for dusting

SHOT GLASS
100ml raspberry coulis (thickened)
100g fresh raspberries
1 jar good quality lemon curd
100g crème fraiche
1 lemon, juiced & zested
60g crushed chocolate cookie
20g icing sugar

SAUCE
200ml raspberry coulis
5ml rose essence

TUILE BISCUIT
10g icing sugar
10g melted butter (unsalted)
10g plain flour
10g egg white

METHOD:

BROWNIE
Grease 6″ push bottom flan mould. Melt the chocolate and butter gently in the microwave. Whisk the eggs and sugar and add to the chocolate mix. Combine all other ingredients and pour into a mould. Place in a pre-heated oven 160°C/Gas Mark 6 for 30 minutes until firm to touch.

SORBET
Boil and place in sorbet machine.

SHOT GLASS
Mix the raspberries and thickened coulis and place in bottom of shot glass. Pipe on lemon curd. Mix crème fraiche, lemon zest, juice and icing sugar and pipe on top of lemon curd. Sprinkle with crushed cookies.

TUILE BISCUIT
Combine all ingredients and stencil required shape on silicon paper, sprinkle with poppy seeds and bake at 190°C/Gas Mark 8 for 6-8 minutes until golden brown, allow to cool. Assemble as picture.

Matt Owens
Executive Pastry Chef

CINNAMON CLUB, LONDON

The Old Westminster Library, 30-32 Great Smith Street, London, SW1P 3BU. Telephone: 020 7222 2555

CHEF SAYS...

VIVEK SINGH IS THE EXECUTIVE CHEF FOR THE CINNAMON CLUB

" Very few Indian restaurants use pigeon, rabbit, or for that matter any type of game on their menu. Indian cooking had a tradition of cooking with rabbit, pigeon, fowl and other less common species. "

Vivek Singh

TANDOORI BREAST OF SQUAB PIGEON

SERVES: 4
PREPARATION TIME: 45 MINUTES
COOKING TIME: 15 MINUTES

INGREDIENTS:
FOR THE BREASTS
1ST MARINATION
2 pigeons, breasts de-boned but with the skin and the leg, liver and heart minced
1 teaspoon ginger paste
1 teaspoon garlic paste
1 teaspoon salt
1 teaspoon chilli powder
1/2 lemon juice
2ND MARINATION
1/2 onion fried and blended into a paste
1 tablespoon yoghurt
1/2 teaspoon garam masala
1/2 teaspoon salt
1 tablespoon oil
FOR THE KEBABS
1 tablespoon oil
1/4 teaspoon royal cumin
1 finely chopped medium sized onion
1/4 teaspoon chilli powder
1/4 teaspoon ground roasted cumin
1 small beetroot boiled, peeled and finely chopped
1/2 inch of ginger, finely chopped
2 chopped green chillies

1 tablespoon salt
1 sprig of mint, shredded
1/4 teaspoon garam masala
1 egg
Breadcrumbs

METHOD:
Pat dry the breasts and marinate with ginger paste, garlic paste, chilli powder, salt and lemon juice and leave for 20 minutes. Sear them in a hot pan for 2 minutes either side, skin side first. Then add the second marinade and finish in 200°C oven for 5 minutes.

FOR THE KEBAB
Heat the oil in a pan, add the royal cumin seeds and when they crackle, add the chopped onions and sauté till golden brown. Add the minced pigeon and beetroot and sauté for 3 minutes, then add the red chilli powder and the cumin powder and cook further till the mixture is almost dry. Add the ginger, green chilli, the mint and salt.

Allow the mixture to cool. Shape the mince into four cakes. Dip them in an egg batter, then roll them in breadcrumbs and deep fry till golden brown and serve alongside the breast.

Vivek Singh

Vivek Singh
Executive Chef

BRASSERIE MAX, COVENT GARDEN HOTEL

10 Monmouth Street, London, WC2H 9HB. Telephone: 020 7806 1000 Fax: 020 7806 1100 Email: covent@firmdalehotels.com Online: www.firmdalehotels.com

CUMIN AND TOMATO BRAISED CORNISH LAMB RUMP, GLAZED BLACK FIG

INGREDIENTS:
4 160g lamb rumps
Marinated with:
1 teaspoon ground cumin
1 teaspoon ground coriander
Pinch of salt
FIG AND TOMATO SAUCE
60g dried black figs, sliced
2 banana shallots, diced
1 clove of garlic, crushed
1 small tin of plum tomatoes, lightly chopped
100ml sunflower oil
200g cous cous
BUTTER SAUCE
1 organic lemon
100g unsalted butter, diced
GARNISH
2 black figs, cut in half and drizzled with blossom
honey, grill till soft
Lamb jus, gravy or olive oil
1 bunch of watercress

METHOD:
Leave for at least 4 hours to marinate but the longer the better. Take lamb out of fridge 1 hour before cooking to come to room temperature.

FIG AND TOMATO SAUCE
Add oil to thick based saucepan, add shallot, garlic, cook on a low heat until transparent, add figs and tomatoes and cook on a low heat, until when you put a little on a plate no water runs from the sauce.

COUS COUS
Cover with marigold vegetable stock and cling film, leave until tender, keep warm until needed.

BUTTER SAUCE
Zest and juice the lemon, place in a saucepan heat lightly and whisk in the chilled butter until butter sauce is made, keep warm until needed.

SERVICE
Cook the lamb in a hot pan skin side down until the fat is a golden colour, pour away excess fat or keep for roasting potatoes, when golden on the skin turn and repeat till sealed all over. When this is done add fig and tomato sauce and cook the lamb in the oven covered with a little grease proof paper and silver foil. Cook for 12 to 15 minutes at 175°C, take out and rest in the sauce. Put cous cous on a warm plate with a little of the fig and tomato sauce. Slice the lamb and place on top, add the grilled fig, watercress and lamb jus, sprinkle with a little Maldon sea salt.

Paul Shields
Head Chef

Paul Shields

CHEF SAYS...
PAUL SHIELDS IS HEAD CHEF FOR BRASSERIE MAX, COVENT GARDEN HOTEL

" The dry marinade is also good with chicken or cod fillet, slow cooked in the fig sauce. "

COVENT GARDEN HOTEL

ALAN COXON

Online: www.alancoxon.com

CHEF SAYS...

ALAN COXON TV CHEF

" **For a different flavoured cream, try alternative flavourings, such as lime or ginger cordial.** "

ROAST PINEAPPLE WITH SZECHUAN PEPPER

SERVES: 4

INGREDIENTS:
45ml brown sugar
60g sultanas
100g unsalted butter
45ml white rum
2.5ml ground allspice
10ml fresh coarsely ground Szechuan pepper
1 large stick lemon grass or long stick cinnamon
1 medium pineapple, peeled and cored
ELDERFLOWER CREAM
15ml icing sugar
60ml elderflower cordial
280ml double cream

METHOD:
Prepare the coals on the barbecue or preheat the oven to 180°C. Mix together all the ingredients, with the exception of the lemon grass and pineapple, until well combined (using your hands helps to bring the ingredients together, as the warmth gently softens the butter).

Slice the pineapple into equal circular slices and put back together again, sandwiching the slices with the flavoured butter. Insert the lemon grass into the centre to flavour and hold the pineapple together. Wrap tightly in foil and place in the oven (or beside hot coals).

Cook for 20-25 minutes, depending on the size and ripeness of the pineapple. While the pineapple is in the oven, prepare the elderflower cream. Dissolve the icing sugar in the elderflower cordial.

Whisk the double cream until it holds a peak (ensure that the cream is well chilled and do not over whisk). Pour the elderflower cordial into the cream and stir well.

Serve the pineapple slices with a dollop of natural yoghurt, elderflower cream or vanilla ice cream.

Alan Coxon
TV Chef

EMBASSY, LONDON

29 Old Burlington Street, London, W1S 3AN. Telephone: 020 7851 0956

LOBSTER, SPRING ONIONS & THAI SHALLOTS WITH MISO BROTH

INGREDIENTS:
- 4 x 1lb native lobsters
- 1 tablespoon golden miso
- 1/2 tablespoon dashi with seaweed
- 1/2 tablespoon dashi
- 1 litre of water
- 8 spring onions
- 12 Thai shallots
- 12 leaved Bok Choi
- 4 carrots
- 24 mange tout
- 1 bunch Thai asparagus
- 1 piece of ginger
- 1 white radish

METHOD:

BLANCHING THE LOBSTER
Place the lobster into a pan of cold water, and cook for approximately 6-8 minutes. Remove the lobster and cool down with some iced water. When cold remove all the meat (tail, claws and knuckles) and leave whole. Set aside.

MISO BROTH
Bring to the boil the 1 litre of water. Add to this the golden miso and both dashi. Remove straight away from the heat, allow to cool.

GARNISH
Cut the carrots, white radish, mange tout and ginger into baton lengths. Cook the Bok Choi, Thai asparagus, carrots, mange tout and white radish very quickly for a few seconds in boiling, salted water. Now plunge into iced water. Remove and dry the vegetables on some kitchen paper (it is very important to keep the vegetables very crisp).

Cut the spring onions and Thai shallots very thinly, wash in some iced water to remove the harsh taste. Dry.

ASSEMBLE
Slowly heat the lobster with a little of the miso broth. Do not boil! Reheat all the vegetables except the spring onion and shallots with a little more of the broth, keep crisp. Arrange the spring onions and Thai shallots into a large bowl. Season the lobster and place on top. Place the rest of the garnish neatly on top. To finish, pour over a small amount of miso broth.

Garry Hollihead
Head Chef

Garry Hollihead

CHEF SAYS...
GARRY HOLLIHEAD IS HEAD CHEF FOR THE EMBASSY

" Being a father myself, I'm really pleased to be involved with this project and hope the book becomes a best seller! "

CHEF SAYS...
AARON CRAZE A GRADUATE OF FIFTEEN

" This is a real kids' favourite. The marriage between the pea and mint really works beautifully, as well as the creamy texture of the mascarpone against the crispy pancetta. "

Aaron Craze

FARFALLE WITH PANCETTA, PEAS AND MINT

INGREDIENTS:
100g farfalle pasta (bow ties)
50g seasonal peas
4 slices of pancetta/streaky bacon
1 tablespoon of butter
1 tablespoon of mascarpone cheese
Pinch of pepper
1 handful of freshly chopped mint
1 ladle of vegetable stock

METHOD:
In a pan fry off the bacon until crispy.
Add the butter. When the butter melts
add the stock and peas. Cook for 5 minutes.
Add the mascarpone and cooked pasta.
Finish with the fresh mint and parmigiano.
Lovely.

Aaron Craze
Aaron Craze
Fifteen Graduate

FIORE, LONDON

33 St James's Street, London, SW1A 1HD. Telephone: 020 7930 7100

PAPPARDELLE WITH PRAWNS AND ZUCCHINI

SERVES: 2

INGREDIENTS:
70g 'Pappardelle' pasta
3 fresh large prawns
50g zucchini
10g fish stock
5 basil leaves
10g olive oil
50g butter
Salt and pepper

METHOD:
Boil 'Pappardelle' pasta 'al dente' for 6-8 minutes. Read label for cooking instructions.

In a large pan mix all ingredients and simmer, when ready add pasta and butter to the mix and cook together for 3 minutes.

Serve in a pasta bowl and garnish with basil leaves.

Umberto Vezzoli
Chef/Patron

Umberto Vezzoli

CHEF SAYS...

UMBERTO VEZZOLI IS THE CHEF/PATRON OF FIORE

" The secret is to use only fresh ingredients and keep it simple. "

CHEF SAYS...

RALPH HELLENS IS THE SOUS CHEF FOR THE FISHERMAN'S LODGE

" Ensure your turbot and langoustines are as fresh as possible and you can get your fishmonger to fillet the turbot if you wish. "

Ralph Hellens

ROAST TURBOT WITH LANGOUSTINE TAILS, BASIL TORTELLINIS & CRUSHED POTATOES

INGREDIENTS:

4 supreme turbot (around 120g each)
12 langoustine, shelled
12 basil tortellinis
1 bunch spinach leaves
2 large potatoes, preferably Charlotte
50ml olive oil
Pinch of chopped parsley
Pinch of chopped garlic
FOR THE SAUCE
1/2 gall langoustine shells, crushed
200ml brandy
200ml white wine
300g small dice of carrot, onion, celery,
leek and fennel
2 cloves garlic, chopped
500ml fish stock
3 teaspoons tomato purée
Bouquet garni of thyme, bay leaf, parsley stalks
100ml olive oil
FOR THE PASTA DOUGH
275g strong white flour
3 egg yolks
2 eggs
1/2 teaspoon olive oil
Pinch of salt
PASTA FILLING
50g white fish mousse
20g bunched chopped basil

METHOD:

Put the olive oil into a pan and heat until very hot. Sear the langoustine shells for a few minutes. Remove from pan. Sauté the vegetables and garlic for a few minutes. Put shells back in pan, add purée, then brandy reduce to syrup then repeat with wine. Add stock and bouquet garni. Bring to boil and simmer for 15-20 minutes. Pass through muslin cloth. Return to pan and reduce to sauce consistency.

FOR THE PASTA DOUGH

To make the dough, combine ingredients in blender. Wrap dough in cling film and rest in fridge. When making tortellinis fill each one with 1/2 teaspoon of mousse and basil. Cook for one minute in boiling salted water.

CRUSHED POTATOES

Boil potatoes and drain, crush with fork whilst still hot, add the garlic, olive oil and parsley. Season. Roast turbot in oven at 200°C for about 4 minutes or until just cooked. Meanwhile lightly sauté langoustines in butter.

ASSEMBLING THE FISH

Place a 1/4 of crushed potato onto plate (centre). Place langoustines, tortellinis and blanched spinach leaves around. Sit the turbot on top. Spoon sauce around fish.

Ralph Hellens
Sous Chef

39

FISCHER'S BASLOW HALL, BASLOW

Calver Road, Baslow, Derbyshire, DE45 1RR. Email: m.s@fischers-baslowhall.co.uk Online: www.fischers-baslowhall.co.uk

CHEF SAYS...

RUPERT ROWLEY IS THE HEAD CHEF FOR FISCHER'S BASLOW HALL

" This is a great marinade that can be used for a variety of fish and lighter meats. Try it with baby poussin, chicken or lobster. The rice can be part cooked and then finished in a matter of minutes. "

Rupert Rowley

THAI STYLE KING PRAWNS WITH COCONUT RICE

SERVES: 4

INGREDIENTS:

FOR THE MARINADE
1 tablespoon Knorr Madras curry paste
1 clove crushed garlic
10g crushed fresh ginger root
1 stick finely chopped lemon grass
50ml light soy sauce
50ml olive oil
60ml sugar stock syrup, made from 60ml water and 60g sugar heated to dissolve
1/2 chopped red chilli
16 large fresh king prawns, de-shelled and de-veined
FOR THE COCONUT RICE
300g carnaroli rice
1 x 400g tin coconut milk
50g parmesan, grated
Chopped fresh coriander

METHOD:

Mix all the marinade ingredients together and add the prawns. Leave to marinate for 24 hours.

Bring a large pan of salted water to the boil and add the rice. Cook for 9 minutes. Drain, rinse and refresh. Spread rice on a tray, cover and set aside until needed.

Bring 200ml of the coconut milk to the boil in a large heavy based pan. Add the pre-cooked rice and warm through. Add more of the milk as required to achieve a risotto consistency. Add parmesan and coriander to finish.

Remove the prawns from the marinade and cook quickly over a high heat. This could be a barbecue, chargrill or traditional pan-frying with a little groundnut oil.

SERVE

This dish eats well with tempura style vegetables.

Rupert Rowley
Head Chef

SEARED DIVER SCALLOPS, PINEAPPLE CARPACCIO & SWEET CHILLI DRESSING

SERVES: 6

INGREDIENTS:
15 diver scallops
Rocket and curly lettuce
PINEAPPLE CARPACCIO
1¹/₂ litre water
200g white sugar
4 red chillies, cut in half
4 lemon grass stems, cut into pieces
4 star anise
50g ginger, freshly grated
4 fresh limes
1 large pineapple
SWEET CHILLI DRESSING
30g garlic, chopped
35g lemon grass, chopped
30g fresh coriander, chopped
25g red chilli, finely diced
75ml Thai fish sauce
100ml oyster sauce
280ml orange juice
1 teaspoon Tabasco
200ml honey
100g mango chutney

METHOD:
Peel the pineapple and cut into very thin slices. Put all the remaining carpaccio ingredients in a pot and bring to the boil. Strain and allow to cool a little.

Put the pineapple slices in the prepared stock and marinate for about 2-3 minutes. Take the slices out, place on paper and keep in the fridge until ready to serve. Mix all the dressing ingredients and stir well.

Halve the scallops and sear in a hot pan. Place four pieces of pineapple flat on each plate, garnish with rocket and lettuce and place the hot scallops on top. Drizzle with the sweet chilli dressing.

Bernhard Mayer
Executive Chef

CHEF SAYS...
BERNHARD MAYER IS EXECUTIVE CHEF FOR THE FOUR SEASONS HOTEL

" The combination of fruit and shellfish in this dish is heaven. "

Bernhard Mayer

42

CHEF SAYS...

ROBERTO FELORSINO IS HEAD CHEF FOR THE FRONTLINE CLUB

" The delicacy of the sea bass lends itself particularly well to the intense flavours of this dish. Do make sure you're getting the freshest fish possible from your monger. "

Roberto Felorsino

SEA BASS IN BANANA LEAF WITH SPICY COCONUT CHUTNEY

SERVES: 2

INGREDIENTS:

1 whole sea bass (700-800g) cleaned and scaled
2 limes
Half a coconut, grated
1/2 teaspoon cumin seeds
1/2 teaspoon coriander
1/2 teaspoon turmeric powder
1/2 teaspoon poppy seed
6 green chillies
6 cloves garlic
Pinch of salt
1 tablespoon of white wine vinegar
1 teaspoon sugar
1 banana leaf
2 tablespoons of oil
TOMATO RELISH
Fresh coriander, finely chopped
Red onion, finely chopped
1/2 cup of olive oil
2 plum tomatoes

METHOD:

Pre-heat oven to 175°C. Oil baking tray and place on middle rack.

Squeeze the juice of one lime into the fish. Season with salt and pepper, and set aside. Roast the cumin, coriander, poppy and turmeric for 30 seconds, or until fragrant. Grind with coconut, chillies, garlic, and sugar to make chutney. Add vinegar, the juice of the second lime, and a pinch of salt. Lay banana leaf on flat surface, and spoon half the chutney over.

Place your prepared sea bass on the leaf, and cover with remaining chutney. Roll in banana leaf, and tie off ends with string to secure it. Remove hot tray from oven and carefully lay fish on it. Allow it to fry in the hot oil for 2 minutes. Turn fish and place in pre-heated oven for 20 minutes, or until fish is cooked (approximately 10 minutes of cooking time per inch of thickness).

While the fish is cooking, blanch two plum tomatoes. Remove skin. Slice in half and remove seeds. Dice and mix with red onion and coriander and olive oil. Season with salt and pepper to taste.

Remove fish from oven and transfer to serving plating. At the dinner table, remove banana leaf and fillet fish. Take care to preserve the chutney crust. Serve with lime garnish and tomato relish.

Roberto Felorsino

Roberto Felorsino
Head Chef

STIR-FRY BLACK PEPPER RIB-EYE BEEF

SERVES: 1

INGREDIENTS:
160g rib-eye beef, cubed
30g garlic, crushed
80g onion, roughly chopped
30g spring onion, sliced with green stem removed
MARINADE
8g black pepper, coarse ground
10ml soya sauce
1 teaspoon corn starch
SEASONING
1 level teaspoon black pepper, coarse ground
1.5 level teaspoon soya sauce
5g butter
10ml HP sauce
1 teaspoon sugar
50ml red wine

METHOD:
Cut the rib-eye beef into one inch cubes. Mix together the black pepper, corn starch and soya sauce, and marinade the beef for 20 minutes.

Heat some vegetable oil in a wok, then fry the beef with crushed garlic. When the meat is lightly browned, add the onion and spring onion. Season with black pepper, soya sauce, butter, HP sauce, sugar and a splash of red wine to finish.

Serve with steamed jasmine rice.

Tong Chee Hwee
Head Chef

CHEF SAYS...
TONG CHEE HWEE IS THE HEAD CHEF FOR HAKKASAN

" Whatever you do, don't substitute the rib-eye. This is the bees knees of Singapore. Enjoy! "

Tong Chee Hwee

44

CHEF SAYS...

GIUSEPPE SILVESTRI IS THE HEAD CHEF FOR HARRODS PIZZERIA

" This pizza will hopefully give you a true taste of Italy. Making your own pizza dough really gives pizza a different dimension: you can't beat it for taste and texture. "

Giuseppe Silvestri

PIZZA ALLE CIPOLLE (ONION PIZZA)

SERVES: 4
PREPARATION TIME:
20 MINUTES + 2 HOURS PROVING FOR THE DOUGH; 15 MINUTES FOR THE TOPPING

INGREDIENTS:
DOUGH
30g fresh yeast or 15g dried yeast
500g plain flour, plus extra for dusting and rolling
1 teaspoon salt
1 tablespoon olive oil
TOPPING
400g ripe tomatoes
2 onions
4 tablespoons extra virgin olive oil
12 anchovy fillets
12 pitted black olives
16 capers
12 basil leaves

METHOD:
First, make the dough. If using fresh yeast, dissolve in a little hand hot water in a small bowl. Add 2-3 tablespoons flour and mix to a smooth paste. Cover with a cloth and leave in a warm place for 30 minutes.

Heat the oven to its highest setting. Sift the remaining flour onto the work top. If using dried yeast, simply stir into the flour at this stage. Add the paste, salt and then, little by little, add 125ml hand hot water and knead thoroughly to form a firm but soft dough.

Continue to knead the dough for 10 minutes until it becomes very elastic. Divide the dough into 4 equal pieces, dredge with flour, cover and leave to rise in a warm place for about 2 hours. On a floured surface, roll or press out each piece into a circular base - the dough will be quite springy, but you should aim to get them as thin as you can.

For the onion topping, skin, de-seed and dice the tomatoes. Slice the onions into rings and sauté in a frying pan with half of the olive oil. Add the remaining ingredients except for the basil leaves, and cook for a further 5 minutes. Spread the mixture over the pizza bases. Grease a baking sheet with oil, put the pizza bases on the top and bake for 12-17 minutes. When ready, sprinkle over the basil leaves and drizzle with the remaining olive oil.

Giuseppe Silvestri
Head Chef

HARVEY NICHOLS, LONDON

Knightsbridge, London, SW1X 7RJ. Telephone: 020 7235 5250

LAMB OSSO BUCCO, CELERIAC MASH AND CARAMELISED VEGETABLE BRUNOISE

SERVES: 4

INGREDIENTS:
2-3 shoulder cut lamb osso bucco per person
1 carrot
100g celeriac
1 small white onion
3 tablespoon tomato purée
1 orange zest
Thyme
Parsley stalks
3 tablespoon plain flour
Vegetable oil
Fine sea salt, white pepper from mill
250ml white wine
Chicken stock
FOR THE VEGETABLE BRUNOISE & CELERIAC MASH
1 celeriac
2 potatoes
1 carrot
2 tomatoes
1 white part of leek
Butter
Milk

METHOD:
Roll the lamb in flour with seasoning. Caramelise the lamb in vegetable oil until golden, then remove from pan and add diced vegetables and caramelise well. Add tomato purée and orange zest, cook for 2 minutes then add white wine and boil for 2 minutes. Next, add the lamb and herbs. Cover with chicken stock and braise slowly until the meat almost drops off the bone. Remove the lamb from the pan and pass the sauce over it through fine sieve.

FOR THE VEGETABLE BRUNOISE
& CELERIAC MASH
Finely chop the vegetables, except the potatoes, into small cubes, keeping the celeriac trimmings to one side for the mash. Boil the peeled potatoes and cook the celeriac trimmings with a few knobs of butter and water to cover. When cooked, mix celeriac with potatoes and mash adding some cold butter and warm milk until the mixture

has a smooth and velvety texture. Season with salt and keep it warm until serving. Before serving, caramelise vegetables until golden in colour and season with salt, pepper and chopped parsley.

To serve place a spoonful of mash in the centre of each plate. Arrange the lamb on top of the mash and drizzle over two spoonfuls of sauce. Add caramelised vegetables as a finishing touch.

Helena Puolakka
Head Chef

Helena Puolakka

CHEF SAYS...

HELENA PUOLAKKA IS THE HEAD CHEF FOR HARVEY NICHOLS FIFTH FLOOR RESTAURANT

"My inspiration comes from seasonality and I deeply enjoy waiting for the next product - that's when I become most creative. For me, creating a dish is about reflecting the seasons!"

HOTEL DU VIN & BISTRO, BIRMINGHAM

Church Street, Birmingham, B3 2NR. Telephone: 0121 200 0600 Fax: 0121 236 0889 Email: info@birmingham.hotelduvin.com

CHEF SAYS...

NICK TURNER IS HEAD CHEF FOR THE HOTEL DU VIN & BISTRO, BIRMINGHAM

" Roast the lamb until medium to retain moisture and flavour. This will give the meat a better taste and should make it melt in the mouth. "

Nick Turner

ROAST RUMP OF NEW SEASON LAMB, ASPARAGUS, PEAS AND BROAD BEANS

SERVES: 4
PREPARATION TIME: 15-20 MINUTES
COOKING TIME: 25 MINUTES

INGREDIENTS:
4 x 8oz rumps of lamb
400g Jersey Royals
120g broad beans
120g fresh peas
20 asparagus spears
500ml veal stock
100ml Port
80g butter
3 sprigs mint
2 shallots
1 clove garlic
Salt & pepper

METHOD:
Season meat and seal in hot pan, roast in oven on Gas Mark 8 for 15-20 minutes, remove and rest for a further 5 minutes.

Cook Jersey Royals in boiling water until just soft. Pod and blanch peas for 2 minutes in boiling salted water. Pod and blanch broad beans in boiling water for 2 minutes, then peel off skins. Cut off asparagus tips and blanch in boiling salted water.

Reduce port with 1 chopped shallot and chopped garlic. Add veal stock and reduce by half, melt in 20g of butter. Add another chopped shallot and mint. Reheat all vegetables, butter and season. Arrange on a plate. Slice lamb and place on vegetables. Pour over sauce and serve.

Nick Turner
Head Chef

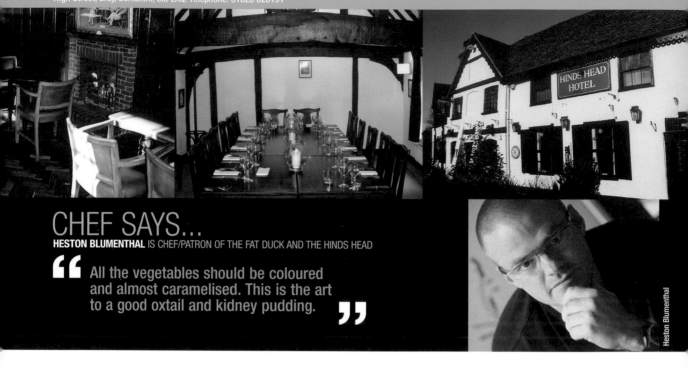

THE HINDS HEAD, BRAY

High Street, Bray, Berkshire, SI6 2AQ. Telephone: 01628 626151

CHEF SAYS...

HESTON BLUMENTHAL IS CHEF/PATRON OF THE FAT DUCK AND THE HINDS HEAD

" All the vegetables should be coloured and almost caramelised. This is the art to a good oxtail and kidney pudding. **"**

Heston Blumenthal

OXTAIL AND KIDNEY PUDDINGS

INGREDIENTS:

BRAISED OXTAIL AND KIDNEYS
5kg oxtail
3 ox kidneys
400g mushrooms, sliced
350g carrots, sliced
350g leeks, sliced
150g celery, sliced
600g onion, sliced
500g tomatoes, halved
1g bay leaves
8g thyme
20 black peppercorns
1 star anise
200ml brandy
500ml red wine
2kg veal stock
2kg chicken stock
SUET PASTRY
1kg self-raising flour, sifted
500g of atora suet
15g salt
600ml water

METHOD:

BRAISED OXTAIL

Brown off the oxtail in a large pan, de-glaze with the red wine and brandy, place to one side. Make sure that the wine and brandy are flamed.

In dripping, fry off the celery, leek & carrot in one pan, the onion and star anise in another and the mushrooms in another. All the vegetables should be coloured and almost caramelised. The tomatoes should be faced down in oil and a little sugar and caramelise, de-glaze with a splash of water. Add all the ingredients together in a pressure cooker. Make sure the stock is melted and the stock is mixed before putting the lid on.

Cook the oxtail for 1½ hours once the pressure reaches the second red line on the pressure gauge. Leave to cool naturally before passing off, reserving the meat for the puddings and the stock for the sauce. Be careful to keep the meat as whole as possible.

BRAISED OX KIDNEYS

Trim the ox kidneys and remove any sinew. Place in a pan with cold water to cover and bring to the boil and refresh.

Place the kidneys in stock with 5g of thyme, 20 peppercorns and 2 bay leaves. This is to 3 ox kidneys. Simmer gently for 2 hours until tender.

SUET PASTRY

Mix the sifted flour, salt and suet together. Add the water a little at a time until the dough comes together. Do not over work the dough. Rest for at least 20 minutes.

STEAK AND KIDNEY SAUCE

Reduce the oxtail jus until correct sauce consistency. Look at Braised Oxtail Recipe.

TO ASSEMBLE THE PUDDINGS

Butter the moulds 3 times, freezing them at each stage. Weigh out 120g of pastry for the

moulds and roll into a circle ¼ of an inch
thick. Roll and stamp out the lids at the
same thickness using a pastry cutter. Heat
up pudding sauce until just melted. Put the
cooked oxtail and kidney into the moulds,
90g oxtail to 25g kidney.

Fill up with the sauce so it is just below
the rim, egg wash the lip of pastry and fork
on the lids. Cook for 2 hours at 100°C steam.
Let them rest over night before using.

Heston Blumenthal
Chef/Patron

HOTEL DU VIN, WINCHESTER

Southgate Street, Winchester, Hants, SO23 9EF. Telephone: 01962 841414 Fax: 01962 842458 Email: info@winchester.hotelduvin.com

CONFIT BELLY OF PORK, HOT-POT POTATOES AND CARAMELISED APPLES

INGREDIENTS:

1kg belly pork
Sea salt
4 cloves garlic
Several sprigs thyme
Duck fat to cover
4 large potatoes, Maris Piper
1/2 celeriac
1 large carrot
1 Bramley apple
200g (approx) butter
2 tablespoons (approx) sugar
Lemon juice (1/2 lemon)
Chicken jus/dark chicken stock

METHOD:

Sprinkle belly pork with sea salt, finely chopped garlic and thyme. Refrigerate for 4 hours. Wash marinade off and place pork in a roasting tray. Cover with duck fat and cook at 90°C for 4 hours.

Remove from oven, place on a tray, leave to cool then put in the fridge to set. Cut peeled potatoes, celeriac, and carrot into 2mm thick slices, keep separate. Cover the bottom of a small roasting tray with a piece of baking parchment. Now you can start to assemble the hot-pot. First a layer of potatoes, season and sprinkle with thyme. Next a layer of carrots and season (but do not add thyme). Add another layer of potatoes season and add thyme then celeriac, season but again no thyme. Continue like this and finish with a layer of potatoes. Cover the final layer with duck fat and place a piece of baking parchment on the top.

Place in the oven at 150°C for 45 minutes; check it is cooked with the tip of a knife. Once cooled refrigerate till set. Peel the Bramley apple and cut into 8 pieces, shape into rough barrel shapes. In a saucepan, cook the sugar until it starts to caramelise, add the butter and stir well. Add the apples and cook gently, this should take approximately 3 minutes. At the last minute add the lemon juice. Put to one side.

Cut the pork into four squares. Take the potatoes from the fridge and remove from the tray, cut into squares approximately the same size as the pork. Season the pork on both sides and put into a hot pan fattier side down. Place into a hot oven 180-200°C for 6-8 minutes. At the same time put the potatoes on a baking tray and in the oven again for 6-8 minutes. Heat the chicken jus in a pan until it boils, add butter to thicken and give the sauce a shine. Add the thyme.

To serve, place the potatoes in the centre of a plate and place the pork on top crispy side up. Place two pieces of apple on top. Spoon some sauce around and garnish with some deep fried thyme.

Matthew Sussex

Matt Sussex
Head Chef

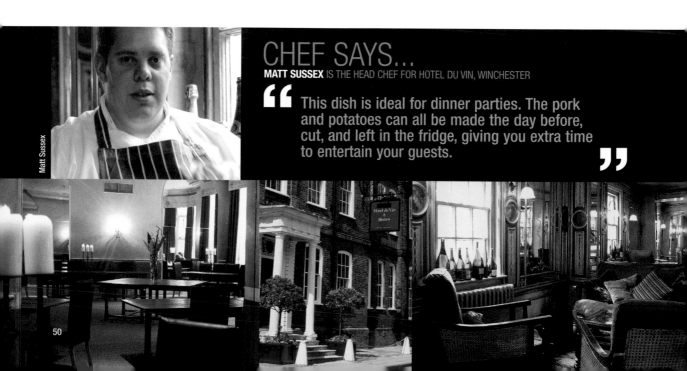

Matt Sussex

CHEF SAYS...

MATT SUSSEX IS THE HEAD CHEF FOR HOTEL DU VIN, WINCHESTER

" This dish is ideal for dinner parties. The pork and potatoes can all be made the day before, cut, and left in the fridge, giving you extra time to entertain your guests. "

CHEF SAYS...

KEVIN HYDE IS THE HEAD CHEF FOR HOLBROOK HOUSE HOTEL & SPA

" As a keen angler myself I would always recommend you use wild sea bass wherever possible. The taste and quality is far superior to the farmed variety. "

Kevin Hyde

GRILLED WILD BASS, LINGUINI AND CRAB WITH PICKLED PAK CHOI

INGREDIENTS:
4 sea bass fillets (8oz per portion)
500g fresh egg linguini
500g white crab meat
1 Pak Choi
50ml white wine vinegar
1 tablespoon sugar
1 teaspoon five spices
Vine cherry tomatoes
100g fresh chopped coriander
DRESSING
Lemon juice (1/2 lemon)
75ml sunflower or olive oil
Salt
Pepper

METHOD:
Prepare Pak Choi by shredding finely across the leaves and stem. Place in an airtight container. Warm vinegar in a pan; add sugar and five spices until sugar is dissolved. Pour over Pak Choi, seal container. Try and do this the day before.

Score the skin of the sea bass, season and drizzle with olive oil, salt and pepper. Place on a tray and grill for about 4-6 minutes, turning once.

DRESSING
Pour lemon juice into a small bowl, whisk in oil and season. Leave aside.

Drizzle tomatoes with olive oil, salt and pepper and grill for 5 minutes. Keep warm.

FOR LINGUINI
Place linguini into a pan of boiling salted water; simmer for 1 minute, strain through colander, return to pan and add a knob of butter, crab meat and coriander, serve.

Kevin Hyde
Head Chef

FISH SOUP WITH ROUILLE AND CROUTONS

SERVES: 8

INGREDIENTS:

1.5kg of fish bones (from white noble fishes such as sea bass, turbot, red snapper, dover sole or monkfish)
15cl of olive oil
2 leeks, sliced
2 medium size onions, sliced
6 tomatoes, peeled
1 fennel
1/2 bunch of fresh parsley
1/2 bunch of fresh basil
A pinch of five Chinese spices
6 fennel seeds
24 slices of toasted baguette
Fresh garlic
Grated Gruyere cheese
ROUILLE
2 egg yolks
1 tablespoon of mustard
100g of potato mash
250ml of olive oil
1 pinch of saffron
Salt and pepper

METHOD:

Prepare the vegetables and roast them with olive oil in a big pan then add the fish bones crushed, and cook until slightly brown. Flambé with a shot of cognac.

Add water (twice the weight of the fish bones) and bring to boil with the herbs and Chinese spices. Bring to the boil for about an hour then rest so the soup can get all the flavours from the bones and the herbs.

Meanwhile, prepare the Rouille sauce. Whisk the egg yolk and mustard, pour onto the potato mash. Finish with the olive oil and seasoning. Keep in the fridge. When the soup is cool, pour through a Chinese sieve and crush all the bones with a large spoon to get a maximum of flavour. Then reheat gently.

Slice the baguettes and brush them with garlic then grill them until nicely blonde. Serve them on the side with the grated cheese.

Frederic Lebrun
Head Chef

Frederic Lebrun

CHEF SAYS...

FREDERIC LEBRUN IS THE HEAD CHEF FOR IL PUNTO

❝ The Rouille sauce and the garlic croutons add a little bit of spice to the soup, which leaves your taste buds wanting more. ❞

CHEF SAYS...

MARK BANDZI IS THE HEAD CHEF FOR LA CAPANNA

" When starting to cook this dish, make sure you have all the ingredients at hand, because the process of cooking from start to finish is very quick and it is important not to overcook the monkfish and mussels. "

Mark Bandzi

POACHED MEDALLIONS OF MONKFISH WITH BABY LEEKS AND MUSSELS

SERVES: 3-4
PREPARATION TIME: 20 MINUTES
COOKING TIME: 12 MINUTES

INGREDIENTS:

2 tablespoons olive oil
600g filleted and trimmed monkfish, sliced into 12 equal pieces
30 mussels, cleaned and de-bearded
12 baby leeks trimmed into 4cm length
2 shallots, diced
125ml of Noilly Prat
600ml fish stock
2 star anise
1 large tomato, skinned, de-seeded and diced
100g unsalted butter, finely diced

METHOD:

Sweat the shallots in olive oil in a heavy bottomed stainless steel pan until soft. Add Noilly Prat and boil until the fluid almost disappears. Then add the fish stock and star anise and bring it back to boil. Allow it to simmer for 5 minutes so star anise releases its flavour.

Put the leeks into the simmering fish stock and let them soften but not overcook. Add monkfish and cover the pan. Allow it to poach for about 4 minutes until almost cooked. Remove lid, add mussels, cover again for a few minutes until mussels open. They will release their flavour into the sauce.

When they are open, the dish is ready. Remove the ingredients with slotted spoon leaving the sauce to boil vigorously. Share the ingredients equally between four bowl plates.

When you have finished, whisk 100g of diced unsalted butter into the sauce and add the diced tomato. Once the butter is incorporated into the sauce, spoon the sauce over the monkfish, leeks and mussels.

Mark Bandzi

Mark Bandzi
Head Chef

JUMEIRAH CARLTON TOWER, LONDON

Cadogan Place, London, SW1X 9PY. Telephone: 020 7235 1234 Facsimile: 020 7235 9129 Email: jctinfo@jumeirah.com Online: www.jumeirah.com

CHEF SAYS...

SIMON YOUNG IS THE EXECUTIVE CHEF FOR JUMEIRAH CARLTON TOWER, LONDON

" Good food is about sourcing the best ingredients that are in season and at their peak in terms of quality. "

Simon Young

LOIN OF TUNA WITH SPICED CRAB CAKE AND ORIENTAL VEGETABLE SALAD

SERVES: 4

INGREDIENTS:

TUNA LOIN
400g fresh blue fin tuna loin
30ml vegetable oil
40g black and white sesame seeds
4 baby squid tentacles

ORIENTAL VEGETABLE SALAD
Bean sprouts
100g carrot, cut into fine strips
100g mange tout, cut into fine strips
100g red pepper, cut into fine strips
100g mouli, cut into fine strips
100g red onion, cut into fine strips

SPICED CRAB CAKE
200g fresh white crab meat
200g Japanese breadcrumbs
1 whole egg
40g plain white flour
4 peeled large tiger prawn
1 egg white
5g chopped fresh coriander
4 spring onion, finely chopped
1 large red chilli, chopped

ORIENTAL DRESSING
50ml fresh orange juice
1 teaspoon clear honey
1/2 teaspoon chinese five spice
10ml rice wine vinegar
50ml sesame oil

METHOD:

In a non-stick pan, seal the tuna in hot oil on both sides (45 seconds per side). Roll in black and white sesame seeds, wrap tightly in cling film and refrigerate.

CRAB CAKE
In a blender, blitz the tiger prawn with the egg white. By hand, add the coriander, spring onion, chilli and crab meat. Season to taste with salt and pepper. Form into tall cakes. (If mix is too wet, add some breadcrumbs). Set cakes up in freezer until firm. Set up three trays with flour, whisked whole egg and breadcrumbs, then put the cakes through the three trays in the above order. Return to freezer.

TO SERVE
Dress the vegetable strips with the oriental dressing and slice tuna onto the salad. Deep fry the crab cake until golden brown. Dip squid in cornflour and deep fry. Assemble as per the picture.

Simon Young
Executive Chef

LAINSTON HOUSE, WINCHESTER

Avenue Restaurant, Sparsholt, Winchester, Hampshire, SO21 2LT. Telephone: 01962 863588

CHEF SAYS...

ANDY MACKENZIE IS THE HEAD CHEF FOR LAINSTON HOUSE

" The quality of sea bass and spending a little extra on ingredients will make all the difference to the final product. "

Andy Mackenzie

WILD SEA BASS WITH TOMATO PISTOU AND COURGETTE SPAGHETTI

SERVES: 4

PREPARATION AND COOKING TIME:
45 MINUTES

INGREDIENTS:
200g wild sea bass fillet per person, scaled and pin boned (ask your fishmonger to prepare)
3 red plum tomatoes skinned, de-seeded and diced
1 small shallot, finely diced
Half clove of garlic, finely diced
5 basil leaves, finely shredded
1 tablespoon finest quality tomato purée
150ml extra virgin olive oil
20g sugar
5g salt
4 courgettes
3 packets of watercress
3g salt
1 medium red skinned potato, peeled and chopped
Pinch of saffron

METHOD:
Boil the potato in some water with a pinch of saffron until thoroughly cooked. Drain and mash into a fine paste. Leave to one side. Make the Tomato Pistou - place the tomatoes, garlic, shallots and basil into a food processor and slowly mix together. Add the tomato purée and mix well. Slowly add olive oil until the mixture resembles the consistency of a Pistou. Season with salt and sugar to taste.

Take 4 courgettes, de-seed and cut into thin strips. Blanch these in boiling water for 3-4 minutes. Remove from the heat and add to a bowl of iced water (to refresh). Dry. Leave to one side.

Make the watercress purée - remove the stalks from the watercress and place the leaves into boiling water for 3-4 minutes. Remove and refresh the watercress in a bowl of iced water. Drain and dry well. Place into a blender and blitz until smooth. Add a little salt to taste.

Take the potato paste and press thinly into shapes. Put on grease proof paper and trim with a sharp knife then dry in a very low oven until crisp.

Sear the fillets of sea bass in a hot pan with a little oil for 3-4 minutes each side. Meanwhile, reheat the courgettes in a saucepan and toss them in a little butter. Season to taste.

To serve, assemble the fillets on top of the reheated courgettes, drizzle the Pistou around the dish then put a spoonful of watercress purée on top. Garnish with the crispy saffron tuile.

Andy Mackenzie
Head Chef

CHEF SAYS...
MICHEL ROUX IS THE HEAD CHEF FOR LE GAVROCHE

" Although it requires some cooking time, it is very simple to make and will leave you relaxed and ready for your dinner party. Be prepared for some smiles and praise when you serve the soup. "

Michel Roux

SQUASH AND SHRIMP SOUP WITH NUTMEG

SERVES: 4

INGREDIENTS:
4 x 175g squash or a 700g pumpkin, unpeeled weight
4 shallots
Olive oil
1 litre white chicken or vegetable stock
200g peeled brown shrimps
Salt
Pepper
Nutmeg
PUMPKIN SEED BISCUITS
200g plain flour
1 teaspoon baking powder
A pinch of salt and a pinch of cayenne pepper
100g medium oatmeal
60g unsalted butter, softened
80g mature cheddar, grated
1 egg
120g pumpkin seeds
Milk

WHITE CHICKEN STOCK
MAKES 4 LITRES
2kg chicken bones or wing tips
1 calf's foot, split
5 litres water
1 onion
1 small leek
2 sticks of celery
2 sprigs of thyme
6 parsley stalks

METHOD:
If using the squash or pumpkin for serving this soup, slice off the top and hollow out the flesh and seeds using a spoon. Otherwise, cut away the skin with a knife. Cut the flesh into very small dice and peel and chop the shallots. Sweat the vegetables in a little olive oil until soft but not coloured. Season with a generous amount of salt, pepper and nutmeg, then pour in the chicken stock. Bring to a simmer and cook for 20 minutes, then blend until smooth. Add the shrimps just before serving. Accompany with pumpkin seed biscuits.

PUMPKIN SEED BISCUITS
Sift the flour with the salt, cayenne and baking powder and add the oatmeal. Rub in the soft butter to make a fine sandy texture, then add the cheese, egg and 80g of pumpkin seeds with a little milk if needed.

Don't overwork the dough, but bring it together, wrap in film and refrigerate for 20 minutes. Preheat the oven to 180°C/Gas Mark 4. Roll the dough out to a thickness of 3-5mm and cut to the size you want. Brush with milk and sprinkle with the remaining pumpkin seeds. Place on a non-stick baking tray and bake for 15-20 minutes. Cool slightly before removing the biscuits from the tray.

WHITE CHICKEN STOCK
Place the bones and calf's foot in a large saucepan, cover with the water and bring to the boil. Skim off any fat and scum that come to the surface.

Turn the heat down, add the remaining ingredients and simmer for 1½ hours, skimming occasionally. Pass through a fine sieve and leave to cool. This stock can be kept in the refrigerator for up to 5 days or frozen.

Michel Roux
Head Chef

LE CERCLE, LONDON

1 Wilbraham Place, London, SW1X 9AE. Telephone: 020 7901 9999

SMOKED HADDOCK WITH SAUCE VIERGE AND TAPENADE MASHED POTATO

SERVES: 4

INGREDIENTS:
4 fillets of undyed naturally smoked haddock, about 120g per portion
100g of tomato, skinned de-seeded and diced
200ml of good olive oil
8 cloves of garlic
2 sprigs of thyme
1 bay leaf
2 handfuls of chervil, basil, tarragon and parsley, one bunch, wrapped in muslin
1 lemon
300g potatoes
100g black pitted olives
100g anchovy fillets
1 tablespoon Cognac

METHOD:
First, for the sauce vierge, gently heat the olive oil with 4 cloves of garlic, the thyme and bay leaf to no more than 60°C. When it is warm add the chervil, basil, tarragon and parsley wrapped in muslin to the oil. Leave to cool and infuse for four hours, then sieve into a jug and add the juice and zest of the lemon along with the diced tomato and the other handful of chopped herbs.

Bring the potatoes to the boil and strain. In a blender whiz the 4 cloves of garlic, the anchovies, the olives and the Cognac with a couple of tablespoons of olive oil, then blitz the potatoes into the mixture. Add more olive oil to get a nice smooth texture if required.

To assemble the dish, gently reheat the potato mixture adding a little olive oil if necessary, warm the sauce vierge gently so it is just warm to the touch. The haddock fillets should be steamed for four to five minutes only, season when cooked with pepper, do not add salt to the fish.

Spoon the tapenade mash onto four warm plates and place the haddock fillet on top, then spoon the sauce vierge onto the haddock and drizzle some around the plate.

Thierry Beryis
Head Chef

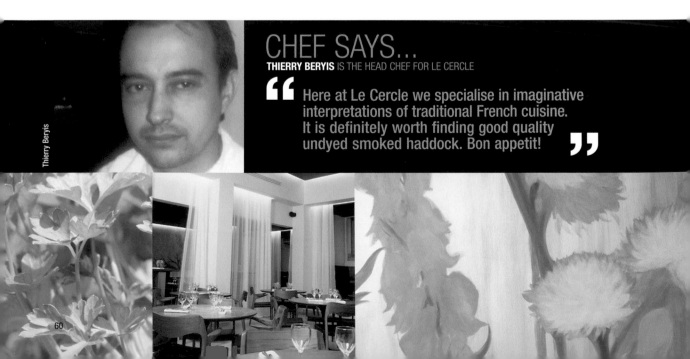

CHEF SAYS...
THIERRY BERYIS IS THE HEAD CHEF FOR LE CERCLE

" Here at Le Cercle we specialise in imaginative interpretations of traditional French cuisine. It is definitely worth finding good quality undyed smoked haddock. Bon appetit! "

Thierry Beryis

CHEF SAYS...

IAN RHODES IS THE HEAD CHEF FOR LE TALBOOTH

" Hand dived scallops in the shell are best to use. They have no sand in them. You can use frozen scallops or those already out of the shell but the quality is not as good. "

Ian Rhodes

SEARED HAND DIVED SCALLOPS, CELERIAC AND PINE NUT PURÉE

SERVES: 4

INGREDIENTS:
12 scallops (4 roes)
Rocket
Curly endive
4 dried apple slices (solution of sugar and water)
1/4 celeriac, peeled and dried
15g roasted pine nuts
50g butter
2 Granny Smiths, peeled, quartered and cooked into purée
Olive oil
Salt and pepper
Lemon juice

METHOD:
24 hours in advance thinly slice apples, dip into a sugar and water solution, place onto silicon paper and dry in a low oven until crisp - keep in airtight container.

Cook celeriac in water and 25g of butter. When soft drain and purée in food processor. Use some of the cooking liquid to thin down if necessary. Check, season and add pine nuts. Purée until very smooth. Store in fridge until required. To the apple purée add lemon juice, olive oil and seasoning to taste. Take scallops from shell, remove roe and skirt. Cut scallops in half and place in fridge. Discard shell and waste.

TO ASSEMBLE
Pipe celeriac purée in an oblong shape with piping bag in centre of plate. Get non-stick pan very hot. Add a splash of olive oil. Place scallops in a pan and season. When golden turn over and cook on other side - season.

This should take 35-40 seconds on each side, depending on thickness. When cooked add a splash of lemon juice and take from pan. Keep warm. Add a little dressing to leaves and mix well.

Assemble dish as in photo with crisp on leaves and apple purée on plate.

Ian Rhodes

Ian Rhodes
Head Chef

LE MANOIR AUX QUAT'SAISONS, OXFORD

Church Road, Great Milton, Oxford, OX44 7PD. Telephone: 01844 278881 Fax: 01844 278847

CHEF SAYS...

RAYMOND BLANC IS THE CHEF PATRON FOR LE MANOIR AUX QUAT'SAISONS

" This amazing, sensuous dessert was invented at the turn of the twentieth century by two elderly spinsters, the Tatin sisters - the world owes them a great deal! "

Raymond Blanc

TARTE TATIN

SERVES: 4
PREPARATION TIME: 40 MINUTES
COOKING TIME: 1 HOUR 20 MINUTES

INGREDIENTS:
FOR THE TART
200g bought puff pastry, thawed if frozen
8 large Cox's apples, peeled, halved and cored with a melon baler
10g unsalted butter, melted
1 tablespoon caster sugar
FOR THE CARAMEL
50ml water
100g caster sugar
25g unsalted butter

METHOD:

PREPARING THE PASTRY
On a lightly floured surface, roll out the puff pastry to 2mm (^{1}/12 in) thick and prick it all over with a fork. Transfer to a baking tray, cover with cling film and refrigerate for 20-30 minutes to firm it up and prevent shrinkage whilst cooking. Cut out a 20cm (8in) circle, using a plate or cake tin as a template, prick with a fork and chill again.

MAKING THE CARAMEL
Put the water in a small, heavy based saucepan and scatter the sugar over it in an even layer. Let the sugar absorb the water for a few minutes, then place the pan on a medium heat and leave, without stirring, until the sugar has dissolved and formed a syrup. Simmer until it turns to a golden brown caramel. Stir in the butter and immediately pour the caramel into an 18cm (7in) round baking tin, 4-5cm (1^1/2-2in) deep.

FILLING THE TIN WITH THE APPLES
Pre-heat the oven to 190°C/375°F/Gas Mark 5. Arrange 12 apple halves upright around the edge of the tin to complete a full circle. In the middle sit half an apple, flat-side up, then top with another half apple. Cut the remaining apple into slices and wedge them into the empty spaces. You need to pack tight as many apple pieces as you can into the tin, so that you leave as little space as possible; this will give the perfect density and the perfect slice. Brush the melted butter over the apples and sprinkle the caster sugar over the top.

BAKING THE TART
Place the tin in the oven and bake for 35 minutes, until the apples are partly cooked. Remove from the oven, place the puff pastry circle on top of the hot apples and tuck the edge of the pastry inside the tin. Cook for a further 30 minutes, until the pastry is golden brown.

Place the Tarte Tatin next to an open window, if possible, and leave for 1-2 hours, until barely warm.

UNMOULDING THE TART
Slide the blade of a sharp knife full circle inside the tin to release the Tarte Tatin. Place a large dinner plate over the tart and, holding both tin and plate together, turn it upside down, shaking it gently sideways to release the tart onto the plate.

Raymond Blanc
Chef Patron

LE MONT, MANCHESTER

Urbis Level 5&6, Cathedral Gardens, M4 3BG. Telephone: 0161 605 8282

CHEF SAYS...

ROBERT KISBY IS THE EXECUTIVE CHEF MANAGER FOR LE MONT

" For me one of the best cooking techniques
is braising. To impart so much flavour creating
the full-bodied, rich, glossy sauce. "

Robert Kisby

QUEUE DE BOEUF REFORMÉ DES VIGNERONS

SERVES: 4

INGREDIENTS:
2 oxtails, jointed (ask your butcher
to do this for you)
125g each of rough chopped onion, carrot,
leek and celery
1 bottle Pinot Noir red wine
1 small bunch fresh parsley
50g tomato purée
100ml sherry
100ml brandy
50g flour
100g air-dried ham
2ltr beef stock (Oxo or similar)
Pinch dried thyme, tarragon & rosemary
Salt & pepper
Olive oil
¼ bulb garlic
15g chopped mixed fresh herbs (parsley, chives,
chervil, tarragon)
FOR THE MOUSSELINE
150g skinless chicken breast
1 egg white
200ml double cream
Salt & pepper & nutmeg
GARNISH
50g black grapes, skinned and de-seeded
15g demerara sugar

METHOD:
Take a suitable size pan, heat, add olive
oil and fry off seasoned oxtail joints. When
well caramelised, remove and add diced
vegetables, return to heat and brown lightly.
Add tomato purée and flour to oil to create a
roux. Pour in 50cl of red wine, the sherry and
brandy and reduce. Bring roux and alcohol
together and add beef stock. Stir until boiling
point. Skim off top of stock and add herb
seasonings, salt and pepper and Lea and
Perrins sauce. Add oxtail and simmer for
20 minutes.

Cover the oxtail or transfer to casserole
dish and place into a preheated oven 120ºC
for approximately 4 hours. When cooked,
remove oxtail, allow to cool. Remove meat
from bone, discarding excess fat and set aside.

Pass cooking liquor through a sieve,
reduce and check seasoning. Combine
picked oxtail, chopped fresh herbs, a little
sauce, check seasoning and set aside to cool.

CHICKEN MOUSSELINE
Remove any sinew from chicken, dice and
place in food processor. Add egg white, salt
pepper and nutmeg. Blend until smooth. Add
cream and blend together (do not overmix or
the cream will separate). Place the mix in
bowl and refrigerate.

TO PREPARE DISH
Take a piece of silver foil, approximately
60cm x 30cm, fold in half for strength. Butter
the middle square of foil, leaving 5cm border
all around. Lay air-dried ham on buttered area.
Cover ham with cold oxtail to 1½cm depth.

Place a cylinder of chicken mousse down
the middle of the oxtail to recreate the bone.
Using the foil, bring the oxtail up and around
the chicken to create a tight cylinder. Crimp
in the ends of the foil. Place in the
refrigerator until required.

IMPORTANT: The oxtail must be cold before
the chicken mousseline is added.

GRAPES
Skin the grapes and soak in some of the red wine and sugar for at least one hour.

TO SERVE
Pre-heat oven to 190ºC. Place oxtail roulade on a baking tray and reheat for 30 minutes. (Check with a thermometer - it should reach 70ºC). Add the red wine and grape marinade and reduce by a half. Add the braising sauce. Reduce to correct consistency, check seasoning and set aside. Remove oxtail from oven, allow to rest for 5 minutes and carve (leave the silver foil in place at this stage) into slices about 4 or 5 cm thick. Place on a warmed dish, remove foil and pour over the hot red wine sauce. Add grapes.

Robert Kisby
Executive Chef Manager

CHEF SAYS...

ANTHONY MARSHALL IS THE EXECUTIVE CHEF FOR THE LONDON HILTON ON PARK LANE

" This is a little complicated, but the end results are worthwhile and visually look spectacular. "

Anthony Marshall

TIAN OF GREEN & WHITE ASPARAGUS

SERVES: 12
PREPARATION TIME: 30 MINUTES
COOKING TIME: 2$^{1}/_{2}$ - 3 MINUTES

INGREDIENTS:
2kg green asparagus, medium size
2kg white asparagus, medium size
100g sundried tomatoes in oil
500g shallots
100ml extra virgin olive oil
10g salt
6g pepper
6 gelatine sheets
60g garlic
1 bunch thyme
1 bunch chives

METHOD:

TO MAKE THE JELLY
Bring to the boil a pan containing 500ml of water, add a touch of garlic, thyme and black pepper. Melt 6 sheets of gelatine in warm water and add to the bouillon. Pass through a fine sieve and leave to cool.

TO MAKE THE TIAN
Trim and peel the asparagus. Cook the colours separately in boiling salted water, infuse with thyme for approximately 4-5 minutes and transfer immediately into iced water to cool down. Trim each length of asparagus to the lengths of exactly 8cm (keep the trimmings). Slice the trimmings of asparagus and sauté with the shallots and remaining garlic, leave to cool. Using a metal ring (approximately 7cm in diameter) place the spears of asparagus around the inside of the ring in alternate colours, use the sautéed mixture inside the metal ring, then add the

jelly mixture in liquid form when it is tepid and pour into ring and leave to set.

TO MAKE THE SAUCE
Finely chop the chives and add to the olive oil. Cut the tomatoes into a fine julienne and add to the mixture. Season well.

TO PLATE
Heat the metal ring of asparagus very quickly with a flame torch (or a cigarette lighter) to loosen the edges. Place in the centre of plate and carefully spoon the dressing in a circle around the edge of plate.

Anthony Marshall

Anthony Marshall
Executive Chef

POACHED FILLET OF TURBOT WITH FRESH ASPARAGUS

SERVES: 4

INGREDIENTS:
4 escalope of turbot (150g each)
2 bunches of Suffolk green asparagus
Extra virgin AOC olive oil

METHOD:
Poach the turbot in a court bouillon
($1/2$ water, $1/2$ white wine, carrots, leeks,
onions, black peppercorn and sliced lemon)
at a very low heat until the turbot reaches
75°C at heart.

Meanwhile, slice the asparagus finely
lengthwise. Pan-fry the asparagus in a little
olive oil in a hot non-stick pan for about 3
minutes. Add some salt and pepper. Arrange
the asparagus in the centre of the plate with
the turbot on top. Spread a fine extra virgin
AOC olive oil on the turbot and around.

Pascal Cannevet
Head Chef

Pascal Cannevet

CHEF SAYS...

PASCAL CANNEVET IS THE HEAD CHEF FOR MAISON BLEUE, BURY ST EDMUNDS

" The AOC extra virgin olive oil added at the end
of this simple dish completes perfectly the
combination of the fine flesh of the turbot and
the crunch of green asparagus. "

MALLORY COURT HOTEL, LEAMINGTON SPA

Harbury Lane, Leamington Spa, Warwickshire, CV33 9QB. Telephone: 01926 330214 Fax: 01926 451714 Online: www.mallory.co.uk

CHEF SAYS...

SIMON HAIGH IS THE HEAD CHEF FOR MALLORY COURT HOTEL

" The beauty of this foie gras dish is that it can change with the seasons by adjusting the fruit you use. We use our garden damsons in the autumn, pears in winter and cherries in spring and summer. "

Simon Haigh

SALAD OF FOIE GRAS WITH PICKLED CHERRIES AND HOME SMOKED DUCK

INGREDIENTS:

2 duck breasts

FOR THE PICKLED CHERRIES

100g cherries, stoned and halved
500ml red wine vinegar
250g sugar
250ml water
12 mint leaves
Bring the water, sugar and vinegar to the boil, add the cherries and mint and allow to cool naturally

FOR THE ORANGE SUGAR

50g dried orange zest
75g brown sugar
1 cinnamon stick
3 star anise
Place all ingredients together in a food processor and process until fine powder

FOR THE FOIE GRAS MARINADE

1 x 500g lobe of foie gras
5g salt
2g pepper
1/2 teaspoon five spice
1/2 teaspoon pink salt
50ml orange muscat wine
Apple syrup
Pain d'épice breadcrumbs

METHOD:

MARINATED FOIE GRAS

De-vein foie gras and marinade in the wine, salt, pepper, five spice and pink salt. Leave overnight. Wrap in muslin, then in clingfilm, and poach for 18 minutes at 80°C. Cool down and unwrap, allowing the fat to drain off. Roll into balls of about 50g. Panné in apple syrup and pain d'épice crumbs. Reserve in fridge.

HOME SMOKED DUCK BREAST

To prepare duck breasts, cover in salt and leave for 1 1/2 hours to marinate. Wash off salt.

Line a pan with tin foil and sprinkle base liberally with orange sugar powder. Arrange duck breast on a wire rack above powder, cover with lid, and place over heat for 8-10 minutes until medium rare.

Arrange fruit and duck breast on a plate as required.

Simon Haigh
Head Chef

CHEF SAYS...

CHRIS TOMBLING IS CHEF DE CUISINE FOR THE MANDARIN ORIENTAL

" The Park at Mandarin Oriental Hyde Park, located in the heart of Knightsbridge offers spectacular views of London's finest Royal Park from every table. "

Chris Tombling

SMOKED SALMON NAAN BREAD WITH RED ONION COMPOTE

SERVES: 4
PREPARATION TIME: 20 MINUTES
THIS DISH CAN BE SERVED WARM OR COLD

INGREDIENTS:

4 naan breads, can be purchased from the local supermarket
2 Spanish red onions
75ml balsamic vinegar
Sea salt
125g Philadelphia cream cheese
400g smoked salmon, pre-sliced
1 lemon
125ml walnut oil
Mixed lettuce leaves, which could include: rocket, radicchio, curly frissée, baby spinach, lollo rosso and chives
30ml olive oil and 15ml balsamic vinegar, mixed together

METHOD:

Peel and finely slice the two red onions. Place a saucepan over the heat and add some olive oil and warm through. Then add the sliced onion and stir for 3-4 minutes. Add a sprinkling of sea salt then pour the 75ml of balsamic vinegar onto the onions. Cook the onions and vinegar until the vinegar is absorbed into the onion. Place to one side when ready.

Lightly soften the cream cheese with a spoon until it is spreadable. Warm the naan bread for a few minutes in an oven and remove when warm. Spread the cream cheese on top of the naan bread. Place the cooked red onion on top of the cheese, spreading evenly. Cover the naan bread with the sliced smoked salmon by laying the salmon neatly lengthways.

Take the lemon and squeeze a few drops over the salmon, then lightly sprinkle a little salt and pepper. Cut the naan bread widthways into five 2cm pieces. Keeping it together, place the bread onto a plate. Ensure all the lettuce leaves are mixed together and chop roughly. Add the chopped chives.

Mix the lettuce leaves and chives with the walnut oil and place in a neat line down the centre of the naan bread on top of the salmon. Mix the remaining olive oil and vinegar together and drizzle over the mixed lettuce leaves.

Chris Tombling.

Chris Tombling
Chef de Cuisine

CHEF SAYS...

JAMES MARTIN

" The flavours released by the combination of the chocolate, almonds and pistachios make this a recipe you'll want to use many times. "

James Martin

HOT CHOCOLATE AND RUM FONDANT

INGREDIENTS:
200g dark chocolate, with at least
60% cocoa solids
100g butter
35g ground almonds
2 large eggs, separated
35g cornflour
85g caster sugar
75g pistachio nuts, roughly chopped
and peeled
GARNISH
Vanilla ice cream
Fresh mint
Tuile biscuits
Hot chocolate sauce

METHOD:
Finely grate 40g of the chocolate and set aside. Melt half the butter and brush liberally all over the inside of 8 ramekins. Dust well with the grated chocolate, shaking out any excess. Set aside on a baking sheet.

Melt the remaining chocolate (including any shaken out excess) and butter in a small heatproof bowl over a pan of barely simmering water, or in a microwave-proof bowl in the microwave on full for 2-3 minutes, stirring once. Do not overheat or the chocolate will 'seize', or turn solid. Scrape this mixture into a bigger bowl, then beat in the ground almonds, egg yolks and cornflour.

Whisk the egg whites in a separate bowl until they form stiff but not dry peaks. Gradually beat in the caster sugar. You may like to use a hand-held electric whisk for this.

Fold the meringue mixture and halve the chopped nuts into the melted chocolate mixture. Spoon half the combined mixture into the base of the ramekins, place a rum truffle on top, then fill each ramekin with the remaining mixture. Smooth the tops of the fondants and chill in the refrigerator while you heat the oven to 180°C.

Bake the fondants in the oven for 15 to 20 minutes until risen and set. Serve with ice cream, fresh mint, tuile and hot chocolate sauce.

James Martin

CHEF SAYS...

BILL McCARRICK FIRST GRANTED PATENT FOR A PASTRY CHEF

" **THE TRUFFLEMAN** has broken new ground in every direction with his hunger to share nature's treasure, the 'truffle', and it is at its peak in this truffle Brioche. "

Bill McCarrick

TRUFFLE BRIOCHE

INGREDIENTS:

TRUFFLE MIX
50g fresh white or black truffle
BRIOCHE DOUGH
450g flour, strong bread
30g fresh yeast
180g whole eggs
100g milk
45g sugar
10g salt
275g butter
10g white sesame seeds

METHOD:

TRUFFLE MIX
Chopped fine in a little sea salt and olive oil. Spoon on top of dough before baking.

BRIOCHE DOUGH
Combine the flour and yeast. Add the eggs, milk, sugar, and salt and mix on low speed for 4 minutes.

Gradually add the butter, with the mixer running at medium speed, scraping down the sides of the bowl as necessary. After the butter has been fully incorporated, mix on medium speed for 15 minutes or until the dough begins to pull away from the sides of the bowl.

Place the dough on a sheet pan that has been lined with parchment and greased. Cover tightly with plastic wrap and refrigerate overnight.

Weigh out 10g portions of the dough. Roll each into balls and place on a baking tray lined with parchment.

Place in a warm and moist area for the dough to rise and double in size. Spoon a little of the truffle mix into centre of each brioche.

Bake at 190°C for 12-15 minutes. Serve to oohhhs and aahhhs!!!!

Bill McCarrick

MARKS AND SPENCER

Marks & Spencer, Victoria, London. Telephone: 020 8718 4904

VICTORIA PLUM AND ALMOND TART

INGREDIENTS:

PASTRY
150g butter
200g icing sugar
250g flour
2 free range egg yolks
2 tablespoons iced water
Pinch of salt
FILLING
250g ground almonds
200g butter
200g caster sugar
2 large free range eggs
6 plums, halved and de-stoned,
or 200g blueberries
1 tablespoon caster sugar
Handful of flaked almonds

METHOD:

PASTRY
Cream together the butter and icing sugar in a food processor. Pulse in the flour and egg and add water to form a dough.

Press into a 10″-11″ loose based flan ring and pop in the freezer to harden. Bake for 20 minutes at 180°C/350°F/Gas Mark 4. For extra crisp pastry, brush pastry with egg white for the final 5 minutes.

FILLING
Cream butter and sugar together, add the almonds and free range eggs. Sprinkle remaining sugar on the prepared fruit.

Pour the almond batter into the pre-baked flan case. Gently place the fruit on top (it should sink into the mixture a little but still be showing) and sprinkle with flaked almonds.

Bake for 45 minutes at 180°C/350°F/Gas Mark 4. Serve warm with Channel Island cream and enjoy!

Fiona Moore

Fiona Moore
Head of Food Product Development

Fiona Moore

CHEF SAYS...

FIONA MOORE IS HEAD OF FOOD PRODUCT DEVELOPMENT FOR MARKS AND SPENCER

" My nanna was always baking and I'd like to think that a little bit of her talent rubbed off on me! This is a delicious dessert that you can make with any soft fruit in season. "

MASTER BUILDER'S HOUSE HOTEL, BEAULIEU

Buckler's Hard, Beaulieu, Hampshire, SO42 7XB. Telephone: 01590 616253 Email: res@themasterbuilders.co.uk Online: www.themasterbuilders.co.uk

CHEF SAYS...

DENIS NOEL RHODEN IS HEAD CHEF FOR MASTER BUILDER'S HOUSE HOTEL

" When the pale meringue has formed, folding in the hazelnuts is the most important part of the recipe, so getting this right is important. "

Denis Noel Rhoden

HAZELNUT CHOCOLATE GANACHE WITH KUMQUAT COMPOTE

SERVES: 10

INGREDIENTS:
GANACHE
300g hazelnut chocolate
300g whipping cream
JAPONNAIS BISCUIT
100g egg white
125g sugar
125g ground hazelnuts
KUMQUAT COMPOTE
200g kumquats
200g sugar
250g water
1 vanilla pod

METHOD:
Boil the cream and pour over the chocolate, whisking until it lightens in colour. Whisk together the egg whites and sugar until they form a pale meringue, then fold in the hazelnuts. Spread the mix thinly on a baking sheet and bake for five minutes at 170°C then leave to cool, cutting the biscuit into strips while still warm. Layer the terrine mould with alternate layers of Japonnais and Ganache until it is full, then smooth the top of the mould and leave in the fridge ready to serve.

KUMQUAT COMPOTE
Boil all the ingredients together until the sauce thickens, then remove the vanilla pod and set aside ready for use.

Denis Noel Rhoden
Head Chef

MJU RESTAURANT & COCKTAIL BAR, LONDON

Millennium Hotel London Knightsbridge, 17 Sloane Street, London, SW1X 9NU. Telephone: 020 7201 6330

CHEF SAYS...

TOM THOMSEN EXECUTIVE CHEF AT MJU RESTAURANT & COCKTAIL BAR

" Foie gras is a unique ingredient which is now being discovered by more & more people. Not only is it found in fine dining restaurants, people can now find it in gastropubs or in quality supermarkets. "

Tom Thomsen

BRAISED FOIE GRAS WITH MILD SPICE, RHUBARB SORBET AND ALMOND TUILE

SERVES: 4
PREPARATION TIME: 30 MINUTES
COOKING TIME: 20 MINUTES

INGREDIENTS:
350g foie gras
150g chicken stock
200g chicken wing
150g rhubarb
1 star anise
50ml red wine
2 slice of brioche
5ml raspberry vinegar
25g of hazelnuts
15 dates, no skin no stone
15g figs, peeled
1g curry powder
Hazelnut oil
RHUBARB SORBET
250ml water
50g sugar
1/2 star anise
10ml port wine
ALMOND TUILE
15g egg white
30g almond flour
25g icing sugar, 20g flour
20g butter, soft

METHOD:
Cut the foie gras into 4 pieces, not too thin though. Set aside the slices for later. Roast the chicken wings in a saucepan until golden brown, if there are any foie gras trimmings left over place them in, add the red wine. Chop the rhubarb and star anise, reduce and then add chicken stock. Let it slowly reduce until 1/4, rest and strain. In a medium hot pan add the sugar, let it lightly caramelise then add the nuts, turn the mass together then de-glaze with vinegar, add figs and dates, let it confit for 20 minutes and cool off for a further 10 minutes, add the hazelnut oil, seasoning and blend in a food processor until smooth and sticky.

RHUBARB SORBET
Rinse and cut the rhubarb into 1cm pieces, sprinkle with sugar and bake them for 5 minutes in an oven at 175°C, then add star anise, port wine and water and let it infuse for a few hours, then strain and freeze in an ice cream maker.

ALMOND TUILE
Mix all the ingredients together, add in the egg white and stir till smooth. Spread out the mass in any shape or size you wish, place some sliced almonds on top for some crunch, bake them for 3-4 minutes at 180°C and cool.

TO FINISH THE DISH
Lightly toast the brioche and apply the praline paste on it. In a very hot pan, sear the foie gras both sides, take to low heat and then add the stock. Slowly cook the foie gras while turning it and baste all the time with the stock. Braise the foie gras for 8-9 minutes very slowly, season and then serve.

Tom Thomsen
Executive Chef

THE MONTAGU ARMS HOTEL, BEAULIEU

Palace Lane, Beaulieu, Brockenhurst, New Forest, Hampshire, SO42 7ZL. Telephone: 01590 612324 Email: dowen@montaguarmshotel.co.uk Online: www.montaguarmshotel.co.uk

BUTTERMILK PUDDING WITH RASPBERRY COMPOTE

SERVES: 6-8
PREPARATION TIME: 30 MINUTES
SETTING TIME: OVERNIGHT

INGREDIENTS:
400ml double cream
600ml buttermilk
250g sugar
1 vanilla pod, scrape and remove the seeds
4 strips of lemon zest
Juice of 1 lemon
4 leaves of gelatine
Punnet of raspberries
1 orange
1 measure or 2 teaspoons of Cointreau or Grand Marnier

METHOD:
Lightly whip 200ml of the double cream, soak the gelatine in cold water. Whilst this is soaking boil the other 200ml of the double cream with the vanilla pod and seeds along with the lemon juice, zest and sugar. Squeeze all the water from the gelatine and add to the hot cream to dissolve. Pass the hot cream through a fine sieve and allow to cool slightly. Add the buttermilk to the mix and then fold in the lightly whipped cream. Pour into moulds and allow to set in the fridge over night.

RASPBERRY COMPOTE
Blend half the raspberries with the zest of half an orange plus the juice of half a lemon. The measure of Cointreau or Grand Marnier. Add sugar to taste. Pass through a fine sieve to remove all the seeds. Add the remainder of the raspberries and leave to marinade for 1½ -2 hours.

TO SERVE
Sit the moulds into a bath of luke warm water and turn out onto centre of a plate. Garnish with raspberries around the pudding. This dish is perfect as it is, I like to finish the dish by adding a tuile biscuit or a brandy snap, to give a crunch.

Scott Foy
Head Chef

CHEF SAYS...
SCOTT FOY IS THE HEAD CHEF FOR THE MONTAGU ARMS HOTEL

" This particular dessert is ideal to follow a full flavoured robust main course such as game or beef. It is light yet flavourful. "

Scott Foy

MONACHYLE MHOR, PERTHSHIRE

Balquhidder, Perthshire, Scotland, FK19 8PQ. Telephone: 01877 384622

CHEF SAYS...

TOM LEWIS IS HEAD CHEF FOR THE MONACHYLE MHOR ·

 Venison - simply stunning monarch of the glen. **"**

Tom Lewis

MONACHYLE VENISON WITH SALSIFY CONFIT AND GARDEN BOK CHOY

SERVES: 4
PREPARATION TIME: 30 MINUTES
COOKING TIME: 20 MINUTES

INGREDIENTS:
750g venison loin
6-8 stalks salsify
4 heads of baby bok choy
200g chanterelles
30g dried morel mushrooms
50ml game stock
1ltr duck fat
25g butter
1 garlic clove
35ml Madeira
A sprig of thyme
Salt and pepper to taste

METHOD:
Peel salsify and braise in duck fat for about 10-15 minutes, depending on thickness. Season and sear the venison then place in oven for 4-5 minutes at 230°C and allow to rest for 5 minutes. For wilted bok choy; blanch for one minute then sauté in butter and a smidge of garlic.

FOR THE SAUCE
Re-hydrate a small handful of dried morels in the juices and game stock. Add 2 glugs of Madeira and a sprig of thyme and reduce until the required consistency is reached.

FINALLY
Sauté the chanterelles (from Balquhidder, if you can find them!) in a pan with butter, salt and pepper and assemble the dish in an appetising arrangement.

Tom Lewis
Head Chef

NOTTING HILL BRASSERIE, LONDON

92 Kensington Park Road, London, W11 2PN. Telephone: 020 7229 4481 Fax: 020 7221 1246

CHEF SAYS...

MARK JANKEL IS HEAD CHEF FOR THE NOTTING HILL BRASSERIE.

" I think the most important ingredient in great food is passion. I also like to keep the combinations in my dishes simple, the flavours pronounced and the presentation elegant. "

Mark Jankel

SPRING LAMB - ROAST LOIN WITH BABY VEGETABLES & ARTICHOKE PURÉE

SERVES: 4
PREPARATION TIME: 1 HOUR
COOKING TIME: 20 MINUTES

INGREDIENTS:
3 large white onions
300g butter
5 globe artichokes
8 asparagus spears
12 baby carrots
8 baby leeks
200g spinach
10ml white truffle oil
50g dried tomatoes
200g breadcrumbs
1 large saddle of lamb
4 large lamb sweetbreads
1 carrot
1 head garlic
5 sprigs rosemary
200ml veal stock
50ml double cream

METHOD:

Remove the loins and fillets of lamb from the saddle. Brown the bones in olive oil and add 1 chopped onion, 1 chopped carrot, garlic and rosemary. Add the veal stock and cover with water, simmer for two hours. Pass this stock through a fine sieve and reduce to sauce consistency. Sweat 2 chopped onions in 100g of butter. Chop the artichoke hearts and add to the onions with a little water and the cream. Cook until the artichokes are soft and then purée. Blend dried tomatoes with the breadcrumbs. Peel the asparagus and retain the skin. Cook the asparagus skins in some water and butter. When soft, add the spinach and purée with the truffle oil.

Peel the baby carrots and wash the baby leeks, blanch together with the asparagus in seasoned water until tender, refresh in iced water. Roll the lamb loins and fillets in the tomato breadcrumbs until totally coated.

Place the 200g of butter in a pan and melt. Add the lamb loins and cook until they start to become firm to the touch, turning constantly to ensure that they cook evenly. Repeat the same process with the fillets. When cooked, remove both from the butter and allow to rest in a warm place for 10 minutes. Caramelise the sweetbreads until they become firm to the touch. To assemble the dish, drag a line of artichoke purée across the plate. Place the vegetables, having been coated in the asparagus purée, in the centre of the plate. Slice the loin and fillets and place them on top of the vegetables and place the sweetbreads next to the loin. Finish the dish with the lamb sauce just prior to serving.

MARK JANKEL.

Mark Jankel
Head Chef

LUCA SPETALE, THE NOTTING HILL BRASSERIE BOSS, PICTURED HERE WITH HIS FATHER, CARLO

ORIENT-EXPRESS

British Pullman Carriages, London. Telephone: 0845 077 2222 Email: oereservations.uk@orient-express.com Online: www.orient-express.com

CHEF SAYS...

MATTHEW SMITH IS THE EXECUTIVE CHEF, UK FOR THE BRITISH PULLMAN AND NORTHERN BELLE

" If you cannot get Sock Eye salmon from your fish-monger, a good Scottish salmon will suffice. Add the mint to the sauce at the last minute as this will give you a vibrant colour with the fresh taste of the mint. **"**

Matthew Smith

SEARED FILLET OF ATLANTIC WILD SOCK EYE SALMON

SERVES: 4
PREPARATION TIME: 25 MINUTES
COOKING TIME: 25 MINUTES

INGREDIENTS:

4 portions of Sock Eye salmon scaled, pinboned and skin on
FOR THE CASSEROLE
1 red, green and yellow pepper, all de-seeded and cut into thin strips
1/2 bunch of fresh thyme, finely chopped
3 shallots, peeled and shredded
1 clove of garlic, peeled and finely crushed
250ml vegetable stock
100g crayfish tails in brine
FOR THE SAUCE
3 shallots, peeled and chopped
1 clove of garlic, peeled and finely crushed
200ml dry white wine
250ml vegetable stock
100ml double cream
250g cooked garden peas
1/2 bunch of fresh mint

METHOD:

Start with the sauce. Heat saucepan with a little olive oil, sweat the shallots and add the white wine and the vegetable stock. Keep on a low heat and reduce the liquid by half. Add the double cream and reduce gently until the sauce slightly thickens, making sure that it does not catch the bottom of the pan as this will give a burnt taste. Add the peas. After a couple of minutes take the sauce off the heat and blend with a hand blender until smooth. Whilst doing this add the fresh mint. Season with salt and pepper and pass sauce through a strainer.

Next the casserole. Heat a pan with a little olive oil. Add the shredded shallots, peppers and garlic. Sweat off until the peppers start to soften. Add the vegetable stock and gently simmer until most of the liquid has evaporated. Season with salt and pepper and the chopped thyme.

Finally the fish. Heat a non stick frying pan. When hot add the salmon, skin side down. Cook for 3-4 minutes on a medium heat. Season with salt and freshly ground black pepper. Turn over carefully and cook the other side for 2-3 minutes, until the salmon is just cooked or until the flesh is still slightly pink.

To serve, add the crayfish tails to the warm pepper casserole just before serving. Place a small amount of the casserole in the centre of the plate; place the salmon on top of the peppers, skin side up. Pour the minted green pea sauce around the casserole and the salmon. Serve with warm new potatoes.

Matthew Smith

Matthew Smith
Executive Chef

WILD GAME TERRINE FROM THE ESTATE

SERVES: 8

INGREDIENTS:
150g sliced parma ham
500g chicken livers
3 eggs
250g unsalted butter
1 clove garlic
2 pheasant breasts, minced
4 pigeon breasts, sliced
100g chopped chestnuts
1 sprig chopped thyme
Salt, pepper, nutmeg
CHUTNEY
250g Quay plums (from the banks
of the Helford river) or damsons
150g demerara sugar
2 chopped shallots,
Clove garlic
250cl good quality cider vinegar

METHOD:
Line a terrine mould with the ham, liquidise chicken liver with garlic, add eggs, then melted butter, minced pheasant, salt, pepper, nutmeg, thyme, chestnuts and pigeon breasts. Bake for one hour at Gas Mark 1½ in a bain marie. Allow to cool and put in fridge. Best made the day before it is to be eaten.

CHUTNEY
Cook all ingredients until they are the consistency of chutney.

Greg Laskey
Head Chef

Greg Laskey

CHEF SAYS...
GREG LASKEY IS HEAD CHEF FOR THE NEW YARD RESTAURANT

" I harvest the ingredients from the Trelowarren Estate for this Wild Menu. "

86

Photo Mike Thor[n]
Apex and Western Morning Ne[ws]

CHEF SAYS...

NIGEL HAWORTH IS THE HEAD CHEF FOR NORTHCOTE MANOR

" BBC Children in Need is a fantastic charity and what a great book. I've donated an old time favourite of mine I hope you enjoy it as much as I do! "

Nigel Haworth

LANCASHIRE HOT POT

SERVES: 4
EQUIPMENT NEEDED:
HOT POT DISH - EARTHENWARE
DIAMETER 8˝
HEIGHT 3 1/2˝

INGREDIENTS:
1kg under shoulder, neck & shin of Lamb
(cut into 3-4cm thick pieces)
700g thinly sliced onions
1kg peeled King Edward potatoes
25g plain flour
40g salted butter, melted
150ml chicken stock
2 1/2 teaspoon sea salt
White pepper

METHOD:
Season the lamb with 1 teaspoon of salt & a good pinch of pepper, dust with the flour. Put the lamb into the base of the hot pot dish. Sweat off the onions in 15g of butter with one teaspoon of salt for 4-5 minutes (to sweat is to cook without colour in a covered pan, on a moderate to hot temperature). Spread the onions evenly on top of the lamb in the hot pot dish.

Slice the potatoes horizontally (2mm thick). Place in a medium size bowl, add the remaining 25g melted butter, season with 1 teaspoon of salt and a pinch of white pepper, and mix well. Put the sliced potatoes evenly on top of the onions, reserving the best shaped rounds for the final layer. After the final layer of potatoes, pour the chicken stock onto the hotpot. Place the hotpot, covered in a pre-heated oven for 30 minutes on 180-200°C (Aga equivalent bottom of the baking oven) then for approximately 2 1/2 hours on 130°C (Aga equivalent in the simmering oven). Remove from the oven, take off the lid or cover, return to the oven on 180-200°C for 30-40 minutes or until golden brown (Aga equivalent bottom of the roasting oven). Serve with pickled red cabbage.

Nigel Haworth
Head Chef

CHEF SAYS...

JEAN-MARIE ZIMMERMAN IS HEAD CHEF FOR QUEEN MARY 2

" I believe that to achieve culinary excellence we need talent, passion and creativity together with simplicity and the finest quality ingredients. "

Jean-Marie Zimmerman

SEAFOOD POT POURRI IN A SAFFRON NAGE AND GARLIC CROSTINI

SERVES: 6

INGREDIENTS:
12 large prawns
24 bay scallops
12 small clams
12 black mussels
1/4 cup carrot, julienne
1/4 cup zucchini, julienne
1/4 cup red pepper, julienne
1/4 cup leek, julienne
20 threads of saffron
Juice from 2 lemons
6 cups fish stock
1 tablespoon butter
1/2 cup fresh cream
Salt and pepper
2 tablespoons olive oil
4 garlic cloves, chopped
1 loaf thick crust baguette
Salt and pepper
Fresh herbs for garnish

METHOD:
Preheat a 400°F oven. Slice the baguette thinly on an angle. Brush the slices on both sides with olive oil. Rub on the chopped garlic and season with the salt and pepper. Place on a baking tray and bake until crisp and brown on both sides, turning them at least once.

Put the saffron threads and lemon juice in the cold fish stock, bring to the boil together and then reduce to a simmer. Poach the seafood in the fish stock. The clams and mussels will take approximately 7 minutes, 5 minutes for the prawns and 3-4 minutes for the scallops. Add the julienne vegetables and cook for 1 minute longer. Reduce the heat to low and swirl in the fresh cream and the butter. Adjust the seasoning. The broth will be thin.

Serve in a soup plate arranging the seafood and vegetables nicely and pouring the saffron nage over it. Garnish with the crostini and fresh herbs.

Jean-Marie Zimmerman
Head Chef

RADISSON EDWARDIAN, HEATHROW

Henleys Restaurant, 140 Bath Road, Hayes, Middlesex, UB3 5AW. Telephone: 020 8759 6311 Online: www.radissonedwardian.com

PICKLED BEETROOT, MARINATED GOAT'S CHEESE, WALNUT MELBA TOAST

SERVES: 4
PREPARATION TIME: 15 MINUTES
COOKING TIME: 5 MINUTES

INGREDIENTS:

PICKLING LIQUEUR FOR BEETROOT
2 beetroot
60ml white wine vinegar
150ml extra virgin olive oil
1 clove crushed garlic
35g demerara sugar
1/2 lemon juice and zest
GOATS CHEESE MARINADE
300g roseary goat's cheese
40ml extra virgin olive oil
20ml maple syrup
20g chervil, chopped
GARNISHES
30g walnuts
4 slices walnut bread
300ml balsamic vinegar reduction

METHOD:

Make the marination for the beetroot with the available ingredients, please ensure that you don't split the marinade. Keep the water for boiling, slice your beetroot to 2 inches thick and 5cm in diameter, blanch for 1 1/2 minutes in the boiling water.

Transfer immediately in the marinade and let it cool down. The beetroot can only be used after a good 6 hours in the marinade. Crumble the goat's cheese with oil, chervil and maple syrup.

Reduce the balsamic vinegar with beetroot trimmings, sugar, star anise, cardamom and orange juice. Finely strain before use. Make walnut melba toast from walnut bread.

Mayur M Nagarale
Sous Chef

CHEF SAYS...

MAYUR M NAGARALE IS SOUS CHEF FOR RADISSON EDWARDIAN, HENLEY'S RESTAURANT

❝ The dish is made of very simple and easily available ingredients and is highly recommended for vegetarians. It has got varied flavours which, when combined, makes a classic combination. ❞

Mayur M Nagarale

CHEF SAYS...

DANIEL TOWELL IS HEAD CHEF FOR RADLEY'S BAR & RESTAURANT

" I always like to save my best dish 'til last and raspberries and strawberries make a great combination! "

Daniel Towell

RASPBERRY MOUSSE WITH WARM BALSAMIC STRAWBERRIES

SERVES: 6

INGREDIENTS:
200g raspberry purée
50g stock syrup
10g lemon juice
2 leaves of gelatine
2 egg whites
2oz sugar
2oz water
150g double cream
18 large hulled strawberries
1oz icing sugar
3fl oz balsamic vinegar

METHOD:
Mix the lemon juice, stock syrup and raspberry purée in a food blender and purée until smooth. Pass through a fine mesh sieve and set aside.

Leave gelatine leaves to bloom in cold water for ten minutes. Dissolve in a small amount of the warmed raspberry purée, then mix back with the rest of the purée. Bring the water and sugar to the boil and heat to 116 degrees on a sugar thermometer. Pour this onto the beaten egg whites and beat until you have a stiff peak meringue. Whip cream to soft peaks. Now fold the raspberry purée into the meringue and then gently fold in the cream.

Pour into 6 chilled dariol moulds; 2¼ inch diameter, 3oz volume, and leave to set for a minimum of two hours. Heat a large non-stick pan and add the strawberries. Pour in the balsamic vinegar and icing sugar and toss the strawberries until they start to soften.

Dip the raspberry mousse into a little hot water and turn out onto a plate. Dress the plate with strawberries and the juices from the pan, garnish with mint and two or three fresh raspberries.

Serve immediately.

Daniel Towell
Head Chef

91

CHEF SAYS...

GORDON RAMSAY

" Rump or chump of lamb is an ideal cut when you are cooking for two. If possible, buy West Country lamb which yields good-sized rumps. "

Gordon Ramsay

RUMP OF LAMB WITH ROSEMARY SCENTED JUS

SERVES: 2

INGREDIENTS:

2 lamb rumps, about 200g each
6 tablespoons olive oil
1 thyme sprig
3 rosemary sprigs
2 garlic cloves, chopped
Sea salt and pepper
1 shallot, thinly sliced
1 baby aubergine, cut into wedges
1 courgette, sliced
1/2 red pepper, de-seeded and sliced
1/2 yellow pepper, de-seeded and sliced
1 tablespoon sherry vinegar
1 large glass of red wine

METHOD

Score the skin of the lamb rumps lightly with a sharp knife. Put 2 tablespoons olive oil in a bowl with the thyme, 2 rosemary sprigs and the garlic. Season the lamb with pepper, add to the bowl and turn to coat in the oil. Leave to marinate for 3-4 hours then remove the lamb, saving the rosemary sprigs for the jus.

Heat the oven to 200°C/Gas Mark 6. Heat 2 tablespoons olive oil in a wide pan, add the vegetables and remaining rosemary, toss to mix and sauté for a few minutes to soften slightly then transfer to an oiled roasting pan and roast in the oven for 15 minutes.

Meanwhile, heat a cast-iron frying pan and add 2 tablespoons oil. When very hot, add the lamb, skin-side down, and sear until well browned on all sides. Add to the roasting pan and roast for about 15 minutes, then lift the meat onto a warm platter with the vegetables and rest in a warm place.

Add the sherry vinegar to the roasting pan, stirring to de-glaze then add the wine and bring to the boil. Add the reserved rosemary and simmer for 10 minutes. Skim off any fat from the jus, season and strain into a warm jug.

Cut each rump into 3 or 4 slices. Spoon the roasted vegetables onto warm plates and arrange the lamb on top. Drizzle the rosemary jus over and around the plate and serve.

Gordon Ramsay

QUAIL STUFFED WITH FOIE GRAS

SERVES: 4
PREPARATION TIME: 45 MINUTES
COOKING TIME: 30 MINUTES

INGREDIENTS:
FOR THE QUAILS
4 boned quails
60g white grapes
40g foie gras
4 slices of white bread
Pig Cauls or thinly sliced streaky bacon
Salt, pepper
20g goose (or duck) fat
A bit of string
FOR THE PORT SAUCE
The quails' bones
1 clove of garlic
2 sliced shallots
1 litre of chicken stock
20cl of port
FOR THE FIG COMPOTE
200g fresh figs
40g soft brown sugar
5cl raspberry vinegar
5cl Grand Marnier liquor

METHOD:
TO PREPARE THE QUAILS
Cut the foie gras in four equal portions and pan-sear them on each side. Put them aside on kitchen towel.

Cook the grapes in the same pan as the foie gras for about 5 minutes and mix them with the sliced bread (once you have removed the crust) in order to get a paste-like consistency. Stuff the quails with the mixture of grapes and bread and add one bit of foie gras in each.

Tie the quails to keep them securely closed and wrapped in the pig cauls or bacon. Rest in the refrigerator for 2 hours. Pan sear them in the goose fat and finish the cooking in the oven for about 15 minutes (200°C/Gas mark 7).

TO PREPARE THE PORT SAUCE
Oven roast the quail bones, the garlic and the shallots in a little bit of oil. Remove the excess fat, add the chicken stock and let it reduce until you have a syrupy consistency.

Pass it through a sieve and rest for 30 minutes. In a saucepan, reduce the port until half the original quantity is left, add the quail stock and bring to the boil.

TO PREPARE THE FIG COMPOTE
Mix the soft brown sugar, the vinegar and the Grand Marnier and bring to the boil to obtain a syrup. Wash and cut the figs in quarters then add them to the syrup and let them simmer gently for 30 minutes. Leave it to cool down.

TO SERVE
Cut a quail into three and serve on a bed of the port sauce. Add a tablespoon of fig compote and decorate with a fresh fig.

Hugues Marrec
Head Chef

Hugues Marrec

CHEF SAYS...
HUGUES MARREC IS HEAD CHEF FOR RENDEZVOUS

" The dish is as much about the quail as it is about the foie gras and the figs. I do love figs and their natural sweetness which perfectly complements the taste of the quail and the foie gras. "

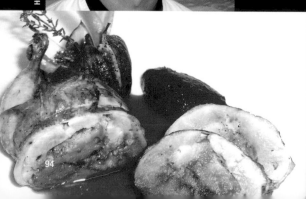

CHEF SAYS...

FRANKIE VAUGHAN IS WARRANT OFFICER CATERER AT ROYAL MARINES, POOLE

" People will eat almost anything when hungry enough. The worms are better left to get drunk in red wine overnight, for their sake not ours. Enjoy! "

Frankie Vaughan

ROYAL MARINES
SURVIVAL OMELETTE

SERVES: 1
PREPARATION TIME: 5 MINUTES
COOKING TIME: 3 MINUTES

INGREDIENTS:
2 free range eggs
1 tablespoon chopped parsley
Salt and pepper
1 tablespoon butter
1 small onion, finely diced
3 large free range worms

METHOD:
Gently mix the eggs together with the chopped parsley and season.

Over a medium heat melt the butter until foaming. When adding the onions/worms they should hiss a bit.

When the butter is foaming add the onions and worms and cook for 30 seconds. If worms are unavailable other meat or vegetable options can be added.

Add eggs and stir with the flat of the fork. Serve when the eggs are set but still slightly liquid.

N. Vaughan

Frankie Vaughan
Warrant Officer Caterer

GARY RHODES W1, LONDON

The Cumberland, Great Cumberland Place, London, W1A 4RS. Telephone: 020 7479 3838

CHEF SAYS...

GARY RHODES

" I think 'This is my Favourite' is a brilliant idea and everyone should buy the book - it's already on my Christmas present list! Well done all those concerned! **"**

Gary Rhodes

GARY RHODES' BREAD AND BUTTER PUDDING

SERVES: 6-8
EQUIPMENT NEEDED: 1 X 1.5-1.8 PUDDING DISH/BASIN BUTTERED

INGREDIENTS:
12 medium slices white bread, crusts cut off
50g unsalted butter, softened
1 vanilla pod or few drops of vanilla essence
400ml double cream
400ml milk
8 egg yolks
175g caster sugar plus extra for the caramelised topping
25g sultanas
25g raisins

METHOD:
Pre-heat the oven to 180°C/350°F/Gas Mark 4. Butter the bread. Split the vanilla pod and place in a saucepan with the cream and milk and bring to the boil. While it is heating, whisk together the egg yolks and caster sugar in a bowl.

Allow the cream mix to cool a little then strain it onto the egg yolks, stirring all the time. You now have the custard.

Cut the bread into triangular quarters, or halves, and arrange in the dish in three layers, sprinkling the fruit between two layers and leaving the top clear. Now pour over the warm custard, lightly pressing the bread to help it soak in, and leave it to stand for at least 20-30 minutes before cooking to ensure that the bread absorbs all the custard.

The pudding can be prepared to this stage several hours in advance and cooked when needed. Place the dish in a roasting tray three quarters filled with warm water and bake for 20-30 minutes until the pudding begins to set. Don't overcook it or the custard will scramble. Remove the pudding from the water bath, sprinkle it liberally with caster sugar and glaze under the grill on a medium heat or with a gas gun to a crunchy golden finish.

When glazing, the sugar dissolves and caramelises and you may find that the corners of the bread begin to burn. This helps the flavour, and gives a bittersweet taste that mellows when it is eaten with the rich custard which seeps out of the wonderful bread sponge when you cut into it.

Gary Rhodes

THE TENTH RESTAURANT, LONDON

Royal Garden Hotel, 2-24 Kensington High Street, London, W8 4PT. Telephone: 020 7937 8000

CHEF SAYS...

NORMAN FARQUHARSON IS THE HEAD CHEF FOR THE TENTH RESTAURANT

" Having worked at The Tenth for over 9 years, I rate my biggest achievement to date as being part of the team that gained their three AA Rosettes. This kind of recognition makes it all worthwhile. "

Norman Farquharson

PAN-FRIED DIVER SCALLOPS SEVRUGA CAVIAR AND CARAMELISED CHICORY

SERVES: 6

INGREDIENTS:
12 medium diver scallops
12g sevruga caviar
Langoustine, peeled with heads on
FOR THE CARAMELISED CHICORY AND ORANGE
2 (200g) Belgian chicory
150ml orange juice
20g soft brown sugar
100ml Grand Marnier
50g butter
FOR THE LANGOUSTINE AND VANILLA SAUCE
200ml fish stock
Langoustine or 100g tiger prawns
40g shallots, chopped
10g carrot, chopped
200ml white wine
300ml double cream
1 vanilla pod
50g butter

METHOD:
Heat a pan with a little oil, add scallops and a cube of butter leaving to cook for 1 minute on each side until golden brown and repeat on the other side. Season with salt and pepper (pinch). Remove and place onto kitchen paper to drain. Add Langoustine and cook for 1 minute on each side.

ASSEMBLE TOGETHER
Slice each scallop into three pieces. Place them around the plate and alternate the scallops between the white side and the golden side. Put the chicory in the centre, langoustine on top, head standing upwards. Put the caviar on the scallops that have the white side facing up. Carefully spoon the sauce around the outside.

CARAMELISED CHICORY AND ORANGE
Place pan of water on stove and bring to the boil. Remove the core of the chicory with a small knife and place in the boiling water for 2 minutes. Remove and place in ice cold water to cool. Place in a cloth and squeeze out as much water as possible. Heat pan to melt the butter, cut the chicory in half and sprinkle with sugar. Place into the butter and cook until golden brown and the chicory starts to caramalise, turn over and caramalise the other side as well. Add Grand Marnier and orange juice, leave to cook on a medium heat for 10 minutes and the liquid will gradually reduce. Remove from heat and drain off excessive liquid.

LANGOUSTINE AND VANILLA SAUCE
Peel langoustine tails leaving the head on (retain the shell for the sauce). In a hot pan add shells and vegetables and cook for 3-4 minutes. Add white wine and leave to reduce by half. Add fish stock and bring to the boil.

Add double cream and season with salt and cayenne pepper, leave to cook on medium heat for 10 minutes. Remove and pass through a fine sieve.

VANILLA BUTTER

Soften the butter in a bowl. Cut the vanilla
pod in half and scrape out the seeds. Mix
with the butter and place in the fridge.
When it becomes hard, cut into small pieces.

When ready to use the sauce, bring to the boil
and remove from stove. Using a hand blender,
whisk the sauce adding a small amount of cold
butter, you should now have a frothy sauce.
Serve immediately.

Norman Farquharson
Head Chef

CHOCOLATE PIZZA

SERVES: 6

INGREDIENTS:
PIZZA BASE INGREDIENTS
15g fresh yeast
1 tablespoon warm water
250g strong white bread flour
7g salt
20g sugar
15g cocoa powder
150g soft unsalted butter
6 organic medium sized eggs, beaten
CHOCOLATE GANACHE INGREDIENTS
300g dark chocolate (minimum 60% cocoa solids)
300ml double cream
To make, mix the same proportion of chocolate to cream
TOPPINGS
Chocolate brownies, chocolate drops, brown sugar

METHOD:
FOR THE PIZZA BASES
Mix the yeast and the warm water together. Put the flour, cocoa, sugar and salt into a mixing bowl and make a well in the middle, pour in the yeast, soft butter and eggs, slowly incorporate the dry ingredients until you start to form a dough. Then gently knead the mix adding a little more flour if it is too sticky or water if the dough is hard.

After kneading for five minutes the dough should be smooth and pliable. Place in an oiled bowl and cover with a damp cloth and allow to prove for one and half hours until the dough has doubled in size.

When proven, divide the mix into 6 balls and roll out into pizza style bases approximately 1cm thick, then bake blind on a flat baking tray in the oven at 200°C for three minutes just to set the bases off.

FOR THE CHOCOLATE GANACHE
Break the chocolate into a large mixing bowl. Bring the cream to simmering point and pour over the chocolate and whisk until the mixture has thickened and cooled. Use within 4 days if making ahead.

ASSEMBLING THE PIZZA
Spread the ganache mixture liberally over the bases and then sprinkle on chocolate drops, broken chocolate brownies, brown sugar and any other treat that you may desire. Then place the pizza back in the oven for a further six minutes depending on how gooey or chewy you like it, the longer it stays in, the firmer and crispier it will cook!

TO SERVE
Garnish with a ball of ice cream, sprinkle with cocoa powder and serve immediately
Note: Bases can be frozen and toppings can be made in advance.

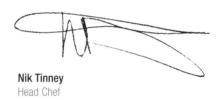

Nik Tinney
Head Chef

CHEF SAYS...
NIK TINNEY IS HEAD CHEF FOR SAFFRON

"If you love chocolate this is the one for you - the combination of pizza and chocolate is heavenly!"

Nik Tinney

CHEF SAYS...

SUSI RICHARDS FOOD INNOVATION

" This dish never fails to impress! It's excellent for entertaining, and is very convenient as the beef can be prepared in advance. It is versatile as it's equally delicious hot or cold. "

Susi Richards

HERB & TOMATO CRUST BEEF FILLET

SERVES: 6
PREPARATION TIME: 20 MINUTES
COOKING TIME: 30-45 MINUTES
PRE-HEAT OVEN TO: 180°C/ GAS MARK 4

INGREDIENTS:

800g thick-end beef fillet
2 tablespoons french wholegrain mustard
3 tablespoons sundried tomato paste
3 tablespoons breadcrumbs
12 finely chopped shallots
2 tablespoons finely chopped fresh parsley
2 teaspoons finely chopped fresh rosemary
2 teaspoons finely chopped fresh thyme
2 tablespoons olive oil
Knob of butter
Seasoning

Thin kitchen string

METHOD:

Tie meat with string at regular 2cm intervals, to ensure it holds together, then season. Heat the oil and pan fry the meat until evenly browned all over. Remove from heat, allow to cool slightly and then remove string.

Add butter to pan, heat and gently fry shallots until transparent (not brown). Remove from heat and allow to cool.

For the crust, mix the tomato paste, breadcrumbs, shallots and herbs together (you may need to add a little extra oil to bind). Place meat in baking tray and spread mustard over. Gently cover the fillet with crust mixture. Roast according to taste - 30 minutes rare, 45 minutes medium.

Remove meat from oven and allow to rest for 10 minutes. Slice thickly and serve with roasted mediterranean vegetables. Goes well with a red Chianti wine.

Susi Richards
Food Innovation

PANZANELLA

INGREDIENTS:
8 slices of stale crusty organic bread
4 ripe but firm tomatoes
1/2 cucumber
3 leaves of basil
1 large red onion
4 fillets of anchovy
4 tablespoons extra virgin Italian olive oil
1 tablespoon white wine vinegar
Salt and pepper

METHOD:
Soften the bread in water, after a few minutes squeeze the water out of the bread. Put the bread in a terracotta bowl. Thinly slice the tomato, onion and cucumber. Chop the anchovies. Chop the basil very delicately. Put all these ingredients together with the bread in the terracotta bowl. Season with olive oil, vinegar, salt and pepper and mix. Put in the fridge until needed.

Giorgio Delli-Compagni
Head Chef

Giorgio Delli-Compagni

CHEF SAYS...
GIORGIO DELLI-COMPAGNI IS THE HEAD CHEF FOR SASSO

" This simple dish to me is the quintessence of a beautiful al fresco summer lunch. To spruce it up a little, add capers, marinated anchovies or whatever else takes your fancy. "

SEAHAM HALL, SEAHAM

Lord Byrons Walk, Seaham, County Durham, SR7 7AG. Telephone: 01915 161400

CHEF SAYS...

STEVE SMITH IS HEAD CHEF OF THE WHITE ROOM, SEAHAM HALL

" This is a fairly involved recipe but is absolutely fantastic. "

CARAMELISED APPLE TART

SERVES: 4

INGREDIENTS:
4 puff pastry discs 8cm in diameter
12 peeled and cored apples
Blackberries
Caramel sauce
Dried apple crisp
Vanilla fan
FOR THE FRANGIPANE
100g soft butter
100g caster sugar
1g ground almonds
2 eggs
20g flour
25ml Calvados
FOR THE BLACKBERRY COULIS
125ml blackberry purée
55g sugar
33ml water
FOR THE BLACKBERRY RIPPLE ICE CREAM
500ml milk
250ml double cream
300g sugar
12 egg yolks
3 vanilla pods
200ml blackberry coulis

METHOD:

FRANGIPANE
Cream the sugar and butter together. Gradually add the eggs. Gradually add the almonds and flour. Slowly add the Calvados. Vac bag and store in the fridge.

BLACKBERRY COULIS
Blend all ingredients together in a food blender. Pass through fine chinois. Reserve & set aside.

BLACKBERRY RIPPLE ICE CREAM
Place the milk, cream, and vanilla in a pan and bring to the boil. Whisk the egg yolks and sugar together. Mix the milk and egg yolk mixtures together and place back into the pan. Stir slowly until the mixture begins to thicken and coats the back of a spoon. Allow cooling and then churn in an ice cream machine. Gently mix the blackberry coulis in and store in an airtight container in the freezer.

APPLE TART
Place the puff pastry discs onto a tray lined with greaseproof paper. Smear a little frangipane over the tart. Slice the apples and gradually build thc tarts up using 3 apples per tart. Brush with melted butter and sprinkle with caster sugar. Place the tarts into the oven at 180°C for 10 minutes, pour a little Calvados over the tarts and sprinkle with more caster sugar. Using a pallet knife flip the tarts over. Place back into the oven and cook for a further 10 minutes.

Steve Smith
Head Chef of the White Room

Steve Smith

103

HALOUMI

INGREDIENTS:
20g rocket
15g French beans
1 grilled tomato
3 char-grilled Haloumi Greek cheese
3 slices of ciabatta bread with garlic & pesto oil
1/2 roasted red pepper

METHOD:
Cook French beans in boiling water for 10 minutes. Roast the whole red pepper and tomato in a hot oven for 10 minutes, Gas Mark 7 or 200°C and finish off under the grill.

When the pepper is cooked peel it and allow it to cool before slicing into 3 pieces. Slice the tomato in half. Place the sliced ciabatta under the grill until lightly toasted. Once toasted pour garlic and pesto oil over the ciabatta. Grill Haloumi until golden.

Place your salad in the centre of the plate and add the French beans on top. Place your pepper, Haloumi, tomato and ciabatta bread around the salad.

Momo Chenoufi
Head Chef

CHEF SAYS...
MOMO CHENOUFI IS THE HEAD CHEF FOR SELFRIDGES, OXFORD STREET

" Mouth watering Mediterranean delight. "

Momo Chenoufi

ST GEORGE'S, MILFORD ON SEA

De La Warr Road, Milford-on-Sea, Hampshire, SO41 0NE. Telephone: 01590 648000

CHEF SAYS...

ROBERT JOHN PARDOE IS HEAD CHEF FOR ST GEORGE'S

" This makes a great first course served in ramekins with granary bread and dill or for two served in gratin dishes with new potatoes and a green salad. "

Robert John Pardoe

BAKED PRAWNS WITH CALVADOS

INGREDIENTS:

28 raw king prawns
2 tablespoons Calvados
60g/2oz butter
2 tablespoons olive oil
2 garlic cloves crushed
60g/2oz gruyère cheese
Salt and ground black pepper
SAUCE
120g/4oz flour
600ml milk
The marinade flavourings and the oil and butter from the baked prawns
MARINADE
2 tablespoons olive oil
2 tablespoons sweet chilli sauce
1 clove garlic

METHOD:

Crush the garlic, mix with the olive oil and sweet chilli sauce add the raw king prawns and marinade for 1 hour.

Remove the prawns from the marinade, keep the juices to add to the sauce. Melt the butter with the olive oil in a baking tray, add the prawns and garlic and bake for 6-7 minutes in a preheated oven 180°C/350°F/ Gas Mark 4. Remove from the oven and set aside prawns, drain the buttery juices from the marinade along with flour to make a roux, now add the milk till a thick sauce is achieved. Place the prawns in the ramekins or gratin dishes and cover with the sauce, Calvados and grated gruyère.

Place under a hot grill until golden brown and serve as suggested. During the making of this prawn dish use fresh ground salt and pepper to taste.

Robert John Pardoe
Head Chef

105

BANANA AND PRUNE ICE CREAM

SERVES: 8-10
PREPARATION TIME: 20 MINUTES
FREEZING TIME: OVERNIGHT

INGREDIENTS:
6 ripe bananas
397g (1 tin) condensed milk
500ml double cream
Juice of 1 lemon
50g caster sugar
150g chopped prunes, ready to eat variety
with stones removed
35ml dark rum (optional)

METHOD:
Blend the bananas with the lemon juice and sugar in a food processor. In a large bowl combine the condensed milk with the cream. Add the banana mixture and then the prunes and rum. Place in the freezer overnight. Stir occasionally until the mixture starts to go firm.

Chris Firth-Bernard
Head Chef

CHEF SAYS...
CHRIS FIRTH-BERNARD IS HEAD CHEF FOR THE SUMMER ISLES HOTEL

" This is a great way to use up ripe bananas and makes a fantastic accompaniment to any dessert. Alternatively serve it by itself with a large dollop of thick double cream or with hot chocolate sauce. "

Chris Firth-Bernard

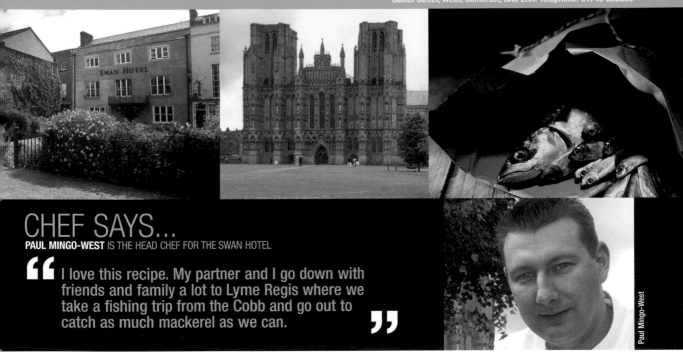

CHEF SAYS...

PAUL MINGO-WEST IS THE HEAD CHEF FOR THE SWAN HOTEL

" I love this recipe. My partner and I go down with friends and family a lot to Lyme Regis where we take a fishing trip from the Cobb and go out to catch as much mackerel as we can. "

Paul Mingo-West

PAN FRIED MACKEREL FILLETS IN SOMERSET CIDER

INGREDIENTS:

4 good sized Fresh Mackerel, 12-16oz
(these should be filleted and pin boned -
a good fishmonger will do this for you)
4oz plain flour
Pinch ground cinnamon
Pinch ground nutmeg
Pinch cayenne pepper
A little olive oil for frying
1/2 pint strong West Country cider
2fl oz double cream
2 Granny Smith apples
2oz unsalted butter, diced
1oz icing sugar

METHOD:

FOR THE CARAMELISED APPLES

Peel, core and cut each apple into 8 slices. Heat up a frying pan until it starts to smoke. Coat the apple slices well with the icing sugar. Place apples into the hot dry pan and toss for about 1 minute until they are caramelised. Remove the apples to a dish and keep warm.

FOR THE MACKEREL

Mix the spices with the flour. Season the mackerel fillets with a little salt. Heat a little oil in a non-stick frying pan. Coat mackerel fillets in the flour (do this in a sealed plastic bag for ease). Fry the floured fillets gently in the hot oil for about a minute each side until crispy and lightly coloured. Remove to a dish and keep warm.

FOR THE SAUCE

Deglaze the pan that you cooked the fish in with the cider, allow to reduce down by half. Add the double cream. Whisk in the diced unsalted butter. Strain the sauce through a fine sieve.

TO SERVE

Place two fillets per person on a plate. Pour sauce over fish and decorate with the caramelised apple.

Paul Mingo-West
Head Chef

TAMARIND LAMB CHOPS, PESHWARI CHAMPEN

INGREDIENTS:
4 racks lamb (3 double-boned chops per rack)
1 tablespoon red chilli powder
Salt to taste
2 heaped tablespoons Gram flour
50ml vegetable oil
10ml malt vinegar
1 lime
MARINADE
200g raw papaya
40g garlic
2 teaspoons crushed peppercorns
1 teaspoon garam masala powder
1½ tablespoons oil

METHOD:
Wash the chops, leave to drain and pat-dry. Sprinkle red chilli powder and salt onto the meat, mix well. Grind raw-papaya along with cloves of garlic.

Cook Gram flour in vegetable oil until light brown, cool and add to the paste of garlic and papaya. Add crushed peppercorns and garam masala powder. Apply the marinade to the chops, leave refrigerated for a minimum of 6 hours.

Skewer the lamb chops and grill over a barbecue or in a tandoor over medium heat, finishing over high heat to achieve colour. Serve hot, with salad and a sprinkling of fresh lime and garam masala powder.

Alfred Prasad
Head Chef

CHEF SAYS...
ALFRED PRASAD IS THE HEAD CHEF FOR TAMARIND

" This is one of Tamarind's most popular signature dishes. The secret is to keep the lamb refrigerated over night in the marinade containing raw papaya as this makes it incredibly tender. "

Alfred Prasad

CHEF SAYS...

RICHARD GUEST IS HEAD CHEF FOR THE CASTLE HOTEL.

"This is almost 'summer' on a plate. Add the lime juice and the zest for a simple, magical experience."

Richard Guest

BRIXHAM CRAB WITH A CROWN OF AVOCADO

INGREDIENTS:

2 avocados perfectly ripe
1 large hen crab or a small cock crab
Salt
Pepper
Lime juice and zest
Fresh herbs (optional)
DRESSING
1 teaspoon honey
1 teaspoon lemon juice
Salt and black pepper
50ml avocado oil

METHOD:

Cut the avocados in half (lengthways), peel and remove the stone. Use a small sharp knife to slice the fruit in 2mm gaps between the cuts, but keeping the flesh together. Curl the flesh into a crown shape and brush with avocado oil and season.

Take the white and brown meat from 1 large hen crab or a small cock crab. Mix together and season with salt, pepper, lime juice and zest to taste (fresh herbs are optional).

Line the avocado crown with baby leaves and herbs. Pile the crab in the centre and drizzle dressing around the plate.

Richard Guest
Head Chef

109

CRAB & LOBSTER, THIRSK

Dishforth Road, Asenby, Thirsk, North Yorkshire, YO7 3QL. Telephone: 01845 577286 Email: reservations@crabandlobster.co.uk Online: www.crabandlobster.co.uk

CHEF SAYS...

STEVE DEAN IS THE HEAD CHEF FOR THE CRAB & LOBSTER

" The 3 different textures and complementary flavours of the crispy onion rings, the succulent halibut and the tangy tomato fondue each work in harmony to create a simple yet unique dish. "

Steve Dean

PAN-FRIED HALIBUT WITH TOMATO AND BASIL FONDUE

SERVES: 4
PREPARATION TIME: 30 MINUTES
COOKING TIME: 8-10 MINUTES

INGREDIENTS:
2 large white onions
50g plain flour
1pt milk
4 250g halibut pieces
1 glass dry white wine
1 teaspoon tomato purée
100g diced cold butter
TOMATO FONDUE
1 white onion, finely chopped
2 garlic cloves, crushed
1 tablespoon olive oil
16 ripe vine tomatoes -
skinned, de-seeded, finely chopped
4 basil leaves, roughly chopped
1 teaspoon caster sugar

METHOD:
For the onion rings, peel and finely slice the onions, sprinkle with salt and leave for 30 minutes. Wash off the salt in cold water and dry on kitchen paper. Place in flour then milk then flour again, then deep fry in hot oil until golden in colour. For the tomato fondue, sweat the onions and garlic in olive oil for 2 minutes. Do not allow to colour.

Add the tomatoes, caster sugar and basil and cook on a low heat for 15 minutes. Place in a sieve and collect the liquid. Gently pan-fry the halibut for approximately 3-4 minutes each side, so that it's slightly firm in texture and golden in colour.

To arrange, place the tomato fondue on a warm plate, place the halibut on top, then stack the onion rings as shown.

Lastly, deglaze the pan you fried the halibut in with white wine, then add the retained liquid from the tomatoes and tomato purée and simmer for a couple of minutes.

Quickly whisk in the diced cold butter and pour around the fish.

*Deglaze - swirl the white wine around the pan to catch the left over cooking juices from the halibut.

Steve Dean
Head Chef

LOBSTER THERMIDOR, MINTED JERSEY ROYALS AND ENDIVE SALAD

SERVES: 2

INGREDIENTS:

1 whole lobster (1½ lb)
COURT BOUILLON
1 carrot, 1 onion, 1 celery, 2 lemons
1 bay leaf, 1 garlic, 1 bunch tarragon
A few black peppercorns
4 pints water
Pinch of salt and pepper
LOBSTER SAUCE
3 Brunoise shallots, fine diced
100ml Brandy or Cognac
200g English mustard
¼ pt fish stock
½ pt double cream
200ml Noilly Prat
100g grated Gruyère cheese
100g fine breadcrumbs
Juice of 1 lemon
Salt and pepper
POTATOES
½ lb washed Jersey Royals
1 good sprig of mint, 1 good sprig of basil
Cold water to cover
150ml olive oil
20g salt
SALAD
2 Fresh endive, picked and washed
½ Head Lollo Rosso, picked and washed

A few sundried tomatoes
Lemon juice & olive oil, just enough to dress salad
Salt and pepper to season

METHOD:

THE POTATOES

Gently simmer for about 20 minutes, depending on size, with the oil, mint, basil and seasoning.

THE LOBSTER

Slice the root vegetables and the tarragon on a severe angle, to release all the natural sugars, split the lemon. Place into a pan with water and bring to the boil. After 10 minutes drop the lobster into the boiling bouillon for 6 minutes. After the 6 minutes is up place the lobster into ice water to refresh. Split the lobster in half, lengthways. You will find it easier to split the head first, and then the tail. Clean the head of the lobster under cold running water. Take the claws and knuckles off. Crack the shell using the back of a knife and retrieve all the meat. Take the tail out of the shell and dice.

THE THERMIDOR SAUCE

Gently sweat half the shallots until soft. Add the Noilly Prat and reduce right down. Pour fish stock onto the shallots and re-boil, then add the cream and season. Sweat the remaining shallots in a separate pan and add the mustard. Pour in the brandy and flambé, (fancy bit!). Add the Noilly Prat cream, simmer and stir until well infused then add the diced lobster, lemon juice, salt and pepper. A gentle simmer will do the trick.

To finish, fill the empty shell with the lobster mix, sprinkle the cheese and breadcrumbs. Grill until golden brown and serve.

David Horridge
Head Chef

CHEF SAYS...

DAVID HORRIDGE IS THE HEAD CHEF FOR THE CRAB

" Be sure not to boil, as this will turn the lobster meat tough. A gentle simmer will do the trick. "

David Horridge

THE DARTMOOR INN, LYDFORD

Moorside, Lydford, Okehampton, Devon, EX20 4AY. Telephone: 01822 820221

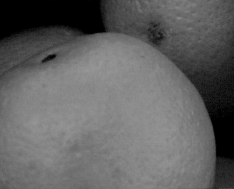

CHEF SAYS...

PHILIP BURGESS IS THE CO-OWNER OF THE DARTMOOR INN, LYDFORD

"Tips of beef ribs are an extremely flavourful cut of beef which certainly prove the truth that the nearer the bone, the sweeter the meat."

Philip Burgess

BRAISED BEEF RIB TIPS WITH ORANGE & A PICKLED WALNUT RELISH

SERVES: 4

INGREDIENTS:

4lb beef rib tips, cut 2 inches thick
Salt and pepper
4 red onions, roughly chopped
Olive oil
1 leek, white and pale green parts only, washed and roughly chopped
1 carrot, peeled and roughly chopped
1 tablespoon tomato purée
4 cloves garlic, crushed
6 sprigs dill
2 large oranges, juice of
3 bay leaves
1/4 pint red wine
3-5 cups hot beef stock
2oz plain flour
1 jar pickled walnuts
WALNUT RELISH
1/4 cup chopped parsley
Zest of 1/2 lemon, finely chopped
1 large clove garlic, finely chopped
4oz pickled walnuts, finely chopped
1 tablespoon olive oil

METHOD:

Cut the rib tips into 2 inch pieces, roughly square, so that each piece includes a bone. Trim excess fat if necessary. Season generously with salt and pepper and dust lightly with flour. Preheat large heavy bottomed pan and sear short ribs until lightly browned. Meanwhile, sauté the onions in a little olive oil in a large heavy bottomed pan until lightly coloured. Add the leeks and carrot, and cook until slightly softened. Add the garlic, dill, tomato purée and bay and sauté a few minutes more.

Place the vegetables in a large casserole dish large enough to hold the rib tips. Arrange the ribs on top of the vegetables. Pour in the wine and orange juice and add enough hot stock to barely cover the ribs. Cover the dish tightly with foil and place in a hot oven, about 450°F. After 15 minutes reduce heat and cook slowly for approximately 1 1/2- 2 hours, until tender.

When the meat is cooked, it should nearly fall off the bone. When cooked, pour off the cooking juices and turn the ribs over so that the bone is side down. Increase the oven temperature to 450°F and cook for 10 minutes. Strain the cooking juices into a bowl, then remove any grease from the top. Reduce liquid by half its volume to intensify flavour and thicken. Check seasoning and return sauce to short ribs and serve.

To make walnut relish, mix all the ingredients together and spread over the beef just before serving. Serve with mash potatoes or buttered noodles and root vegetables.

Philip Burgess
Co-Owner

THE FOX, WILLIAN

Willian, Letchworth, Hertfordshire, SG6 2AE. Telephone: 01462 480233

CRAB, SMOKED SALMON AND SPINACH BHAJI WITH CUCUMBER SALAD

SERVES: 6-8
PREPARATION TIME: 1 HOUR
COOKING TIME: 20 MINUTES

INGREDIENTS:

FOR THE BHAJI
150g white crabmeat
150g smoked salmon
250g Gram flour
3 teaspoons cumin seed
3/4 teaspoon sea salt
1 fresh chilli finely chopped
8 tablespoons water
4 tablespoons natural yoghurt
1 medium potato cut into 5mm dice
1 medium onion finely diced
200g spinach chopped
4 tablespoons fresh chopped coriander
Vegetable oil for frying
THE SALAD
1 cucumber
2 tablespoons white wine vinegar
2 teaspoons caster sugar
1-2 tablespoons chilli sauce (to taste)
1/2 red onion finely sliced
1/2 teaspoon crushed garlic
1 tablespoon fish sauce (optional)

THE DRESSING
1 tin mango slices in natural juice
3 tablespoons chopped coriander
Dash of white wine vinegar
Picked coriander leaves and lime wedges for garnish

METHOD:

FOR THE BHAJI
Blanch diced potato in boiling water until half cooked, refresh in cold water and set aside. Add all ingredients except water and yoghurt into a large bowl and mix together. Add potato, yoghurt and water to form a stiff mix. Chill in the fridge for 30 minutes then form into bhaji shapes and chill on a cling film covered tray for a further 15 minutes.

FOR THE SALAD
Mix sugar with vinegar until it dissolves then add to peeled and thinly sliced cucumber. Chill for 20 minutes then add rest of salad ingredients.

FOR THE DRESSING
Place the mango, coriander and vinegar in a blender until smooth, set aside.

TO SERVE
Fill a deep frying pan 1/3 full with oil and heat to 150ºF. Cook the bhajis in pairs for 3-4 minutes each side, drain and keep warm. Serve immediately with dressing on the plate then add salad and then the bahji. Garnish with coriander leaves and lime wedges.

Frank Skinner
Head Chef

CHEF SAYS...

FRANK SKINNER IS THE HEAD CHEF FOR THE FOX AT WILLIAN

" Substitute the crab and salmon for anything else you fancy, a good way to use a few leftovers and if there are any spices you don't like then they can be left out or replaced according to your taste. "

Frank Skinner

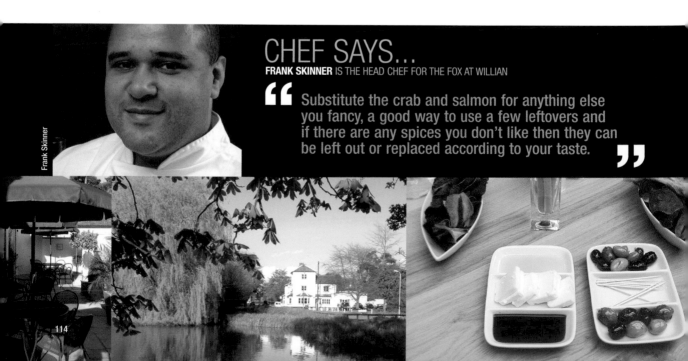

THE GREAT HOUSE, LAVENHAM

Market Place, Lavenham, Sudbury, Suffolk, CO10 9QZ. Telephone: 01787 247431 Fax: 01787 248007 Email: info@greathouse.co.uk Online: www.greathouse.co.uk

CHEF SAYS...

ENRIQUE BILBAULT IS HEAD CHEF FOR THE GREAT HOUSE

" The 'Feuillantines' layers bring a crunchy and lighter taste to the chocolate and praline mousse. "

Enrique Bilbault

FEUILLANTINE CROQUANT WITH A HAZELNUT PRALINE MOUSSE

SERVES: 10

INGREDIENTS:
450g milk chocolate
115g praline
8 egg whites
225g caster sugar
5 gelatine leaves
375g whipping cream

METHOD:
Melt the milk chocolate and praline in a bowl over the Bain Marie. Put the sugar and a bit of water in a pan and heat to melt the sugar then start to boil to 120°C.

Start to beat the egg whites in a mixer. Melt the gelatine leaves in a bowl in cold water. When the syrup reaches 120°C slowly pour it all into the egg whites between beaters. Add the softened gelatine.

Continue beating until the egg white is cold. Lightly whip the cream and mix it together with the chocolate. Then gently fold it all with the meringue. To assemble the cake use a circle of 25cm width by 7cm high and place a first layer of chocolate cream, then a layer of crème patissière, then another layer of chocolate cream.

Enrique Bilbault
Head Chef

SUMMER JELLY

SERVES: 6

INGREDIENTS:
3 sheets of leaf gelatine
200ml cold water
75g granulated sugar
75ml elderflower cordial
125g mixed summer berries - raspberries,
blackcurrants, strawberries

METHOD:
Put the gelatine leaves in a small bowl with half the cold water and leave to soak for at least 5 minutes. Pour the rest of the water into a medium sized pan, add the sugar and warm slowly, stirring occasionally, until the sugar has dissolved.

Add the gelatine leaves and water to the warm sugar syrup, stir in the elderflower cordial and stir well until all the gelatine has dissolved. Put to one side to cool a little.

Divide the berries between teacup moulds, fill up with the elderflower syrup and leave to set in a refrigerator (if there is time, for best results, half fill the teacups with berries and syrup, leave to set in the fridge then top up with remaining berries and syrup).

To turn them out, quickly dip the teacup in hot water then turn upside down onto the serving dish.

Mathieu le Boulanger
Pastry Chef

Mathieu le Boulanger

CHEF SAYS...

MATHIEU LE BOULANGER IS PASTRY CHEF FOR THE HEADLAND HOTEL, NEWQUAY

" Very easy, stunning colours, ideal for impressing friends. "

CHEF SAYS...

PAUL ASKEW IS CHEF PATRON/DIRECTOR FOR THE LONDON CARRIAGE WORKS.

" The secret to all good cooking is to source great quality ingredients that are in season and at their peak. "

Paul Askew

DUO OF SUMMER MARKET FISH

SERVES: 4

INGREDIENTS:

8 large fresh king scallops, shelled and cleaned with beak removed
One 1 kilo wild sea bass, de-scaled, gutted and filleted
400g samphire (or asparagus)
FOR THE SALAD
1 tablespoon of superfine capers
10 pitted black olives
Bunch of basil, chopped
Good olive oil
Cracked black pepper, pinch
4 spring onions, washed peeled and finely chopped
Squeeze of lemon
FOR THE SAUCE
100g butter
1 glass of vermouth
4 pieces star anise
100ml double cream
Sea salt flakes, to taste
Cracked black pepper, to taste
4 cloves of garlic, peeled and chopped
3 banana shallots, peeled and diced
Bunch flat leaf parsley, chervil to garnish
100ml of fish stock, fresh preferably or from a stock cube

METHOD:

FIRST MAKE THE SALAD
De-skin, de-seed and finely dice the vine tomatoes then mix together with all the salad ingredients adding lemon and seasoning to taste and refrigerate.

FOR THE SAUCE
Finely chop the shallots and garlic in a tablespoon each of butter and olive oil, fry gently to soften for a minute or two and then add the rest of the sauce ingredients adding the cream last. Bring to the boil, then simmer fairly rapidly until the liquid is reduced by about half and has the consistency to coat the back of a spoon. Pass through a fine sieve and leave to one side.

FOR THE FISH
Thoroughly rinse and drain the samphire. Season the fish on both sides. Heat about a tablespoon of the olive oil in a good non-stick frying pan and add the seasoned fish, skin

side down for a minute, after which add a knob of butter, turn the fish and cook for a further 2 minutes. Add the samphire to the fish pan and just heat through. Then take out both the fish and the samphire and drain on absorbent kitchen paper.

To another frying pan or griddle add a knob of butter and a drizzle of light olive oil, bring to a very high heat, add the scallops and cook for one minute on either side. Remove the scallops and drain onto absorbent kitchen paper. Reheat the sauce, pour into a jug and foam with a stick blender.

Assemble the fish, salad and samphire onto serving plates as illustrated and finish with the sauce.

Paul Askew
Chef Patron/Director

CHEF SAYS...

JAMIE ROBERTS IS THE HEAD CHEF FOR THE MILLER HOWE HOTEL AND RESTAURANT

" Miller Howe is pleased to support this BBC Children In Need Recipe Book in memory of our great friend and frequent visitor, the late Michelle Kershaw, a Director of Lakeland Limited and Trustee of Children In Need. "

Jamie Roberts

ROASTED LOIN OF KENTMERE LAMB, BASIL POMME PURÉE & JUS PIPERADE

SERVES: 4-6

INGREDIENTS:
2 loins of Kentmere or other good quality lamb loins
Olive oil, cumin, seasoning, unsalted butter
FOR THE AUBERGINE CAVIAR
2 large aubergines
1 clove of garlic peeled and halved
Quarter of lemon
1 tablespoon of olive oil
4 sprigs of thyme
Freshly ground white pepper and salt
FOR THE RATATOUILLE
2 cloves of garlic
1 small onion, diced
2 tablespoons of olive oil
4 plum tomatoes, concassé
1 red pepper, finely diced
1 small fennel bulb, finely sliced
Half of aubergine, small dice
2 courgettes, small dice
Seasoning
FOR THE CONFIT TOMATOES
3 tomatoes, plum tomatoes
1 clove of garlic, 4 sprigs of thyme
1 teaspoon of salt
1 teaspoon of sugar

FOR THE BASIL POMME PURÉE
3 tablespoons of basil oil (blanched basil, blended with half olive oil & half vegetable oil)
6 portions of dry potato purée
FOR THE JUS PIPERADE
1 litre of good quality lamb stock
4 red peppers

METHOD:

AUBERGINE CAVIAR
Halve the aubergine lengthways, rub the surface first with garlic, then with lemon to prevent discolouration. Make a few deep incisions in the flesh and sprinkle with olive oil, place on a baking tray add thyme and seasoning, cover loosely with foil, and cook in pre-heated oven at 190°C/Gas Mark 5 for 45 minutes to 1 hour. Remove and leave to cool for 5 minutes.

Finishing the aubergine: When cooled scoop the flesh from the aubergine onto a chopping board, chop very finely & check seasoning. Stand the aubergine in a small sieve to discard any excess juices.

RATATOUILLE
Sweat garlic and onion in olive oil, add the tomatoes and simmer for 5 minutes, blend and strain. Sauté off the rest of the ingredients one by one until just cooked. Combine all the ingredients into the puréed tomato sauce and season.

CONFIT TOMATOES
Peel and quarter the tomatoes, place on baking parchment, sprinkle with sugar, salt, thyme and sliced garlic. Leave in a warm place for 1-2 hours.

JUS PIPERADE
Roast the red peppers in a hot frying pan until the skin colours, remove from heat, place in a container, cover with cling film and leave in a warm place for 1/2 hour (this helps the peppers to peel easier). Start to reduce lamb stock, when the peppers are cool, peel and cut into small dice, discarding

all the pips, add to the reduced lamb stock, reduce to a good consistency, always skimming, season at the end, reheat to serve.

COOKING THE LAMB LOIN
Season the lamb with olive oil, salt, cumin and black pepper, sear in a hot pan first with one tablespoon of olive oil then add one small knob of unsalted butter, brown both sides, place in a pre-heated oven 230°C/Gas Mark 8. Roast for 4-6 minutes depending on size of loins. Rest in a warm place for 10 minutes before serving.

Jamie Roberts
Head Chef

RARE BEEF SALAD, WILD ROQUETTE, PLUM TOMATOES & SHAVED PARMESAN

SERVES: 2

INGREDIENTS:
2 x 200g sirloin steaks
2 large plum tomatoes
2 bunches of wild roquette
40g toasted pine nuts
Parmesan shavings
20ml truffle oil
15ml aged balsamic vinegar
Salt and pepper
Olive oil for frying

METHOD:
Season both sides of the steaks. Heat the olive oil in a frying pan. Sear the steaks for approximately 2 minutes each side. Leave to rest in a warm place. Wash and dry the roquette, toss with the truffle oil and aged balsamic and arrange in the middle of the plate.

Quarter the plum tomatoes, skin and de-seed. Slice the steaks and rest the slices upon the roquette.

Add pine nuts and parmesan shavings. Drizzle truffle oil and balsamic around the plate. Season with good quality sea salt.

Alex Howard
Head Chef

CHEF SAYS...
ALEX HOWARD IS HEAD CHEF FOR THE OPERA HOUSE

" This is my favourite combination of flavours, easy and delicious, the perfect summertime salad. "

Alex Howard

CHEF SAYS...

ALAN POSTILL IS HEAD CHEF FOR THE PEAR TREE AT PURTON

" Because of the long slow cooking, the fat breaks down and becomes gelatinous. After the glazing process it just melts in the mouth. "

Alan Postill

BRAISED, GLAZED PORK BELLY

SERVES: 6-8
PREPARATION TIME: 15 MINUTES
COOKING TIME: JUST OVER 4 HOURS

INGREDIENTS:

5lbs/2.5kg rindless and boneless free-range pork belly
1 large onion
6 shallots
4 stalks celery
3 carrots
6 cloves garlic
3 red chillies
2cm length of fresh ginger
2 tablespoons of honey
1 sprig of rosemary
Enough meat stock to cover
Salt to season

METHOD:

Place pork in a deep roasting tray, not much bigger than the meat itself. Peel and chop all vegetables then add them to the pork, along with the honey, salt, rosemary and meat stock.

Bring to a simmer, cover with foil and cook gently in the oven for 4 hours on 150°C/300°F/Gas Mark 2. The pork is ready when a wooden skewer slides through with no (or very little) resistance.

Allow to cool/rest in liquor, strain off the liquor and reduce it to a sauce consistency. Two or three drops of balsamic vinegar can be added to balance the sweetness.

Cut pork into slices approximately 3cm wide. Drizzle with a little extra honey and a little sauce and glaze for about 5 minutes in a hot oven - basting regularly.

Alan Postill
Head Chef

121

MICHAEL CAINES AT ABODE EXETER

The Royal Clarence, Exeter, Devon, EX1 1HD. Telephone: 01392 223638 Email: tables@michaelcaines.com

CHEF SAYS...

MICHAEL CAINES IS THE OWNER OF MICHAEL CAINES AT ABODE, EXETER

" Blanch the lobster first for 30 seconds to release the pigment from the shell allowing it to come away cleanly. This allows you to pan-fry the lobster without the shell and serve it cleanly without fuss. "

Michael Caines

FRICASSÉE OF CORNISH OR BRIXHAM LOBSTER WITH SUMMER VEGETABLES

INGREDIENTS:

4 x 500g live lobsters
Lobster Bisque (see below)
12 baby carrots, 12 baby fennel
12 asparagus tips, spring cabbage
50g broad beans, 50g peas
Chopped fresh tarragon
Olive oil
Picked tarragon, chervil and chives to garnish
FOR THE LOBSTER BISQUE
1kg lobster carcasses
500ml extra virgin olive oil
50ml Cognac
100g carrots, finely chopped
100g onion, finely chopped
100g fennel, finely chopped
1/2 clove garlic, chopped
5g whole white peppercorns
5g coriander seeds, crushed
5g cumin seeds, crushed
5g cardamom seeds, crushed
1 star anise, crushed
1 bay leaf
5 sprigs thyme
250g plum tomatoes, chopped
200ml water
30g tomato purée
5g salt
100g unsalted butter
A little lemon juice

METHOD:

PREPARATION OF LOBSTERS

Kill the lobsters by pressing a sharp knife into the lobsters' head about an inch or an inch and a half from between the eyes towards the tail. Press down until the blade goes all the way through to the cutting board and draw the knife towards the eyes.

Remove the tails and claws. Blanch the tails in boiling water for 30 seconds, then place into iced water. Bring the hot water back up to the boil, then add the lobster claws, bring to the boil again and cook for 3 minutes. Place in the iced water. Peel the lobster tail to remove the tail meat and crack the claws to remove the claw meat, keeping the claws as whole as possible. Place the lobster meat on a tray for later use.

LOBSTER BISQUE

Place a roasting tray in an oven pre-heated to 200°C. Heat 400ml of the olive oil and then add the lobster carcasses, roast for 30

minutes (do not let burn) and remove from the heat. Deglaze with the Cognac. Separately in a stainless steel pan, sweat the carrots, onions, fennel and garlic in the remaining 100ml of olive oil for 10 minutes without colouring. Add the spices and herbs and sweat for a further 5 minutes. Add the tomato purée, fresh tomatoes and water, cook for a further 10 minutes.

Add the roasted carcasses and the juices. Add water to below the top of the carcasses and bring to the boil. Simmer and cook for 20 minutes. Drain well, then pass through a fine sieve. Taste and adjust seasoning.

TO FINISH

Heat 200ml of lobster bisque and 100g of unsalted butter and using a hand blender blend until frothy. Season with salt, pepper and a drop of lemon juice.

TO SERVE

Cook the vegetables in boiling salted water, or steamer. Peel the broad beans to remove

the bitter skins. Using 2 non-stick frying pans (one for the tail and the other for the claws), heat some olive oil and carefully add the lobster. Place in the pre-heated oven for 2 minutes, turn over add the tarragon, continue to cook for a further 2 minutes. Re-heat the vegetables in a steamer.

Slice the lobster tail into 6 pieces and dress around the bowl or plate, place the claw meat into the middle and then scatter the vegetables around.

Heat and froth the sauce and spoon around the dish. Drizzle some of the cooking oil around and sprinkle the picked herbs over the dish to finish. Enjoy!

Michael Caines
Proprietor

THE ROYAL OAK, EAST LAVANT

Pook Lane, East Lavant, West Sussex, PO18 0AX. Telephone: 01243 527434

CHEF SAYS...

MALCOLM GOBLE IS THE HEAD CHEF AT THE ROYAL OAK

" Naughty but nice chocolate and for charity is a match made in heaven. "

Malcolm Goble

WARM CHOCOLATE FONDANT WITH A CHOCOLATE & HAZELNUT MASCARPONE

SERVES: 4

INGREDIENTS:
FOR THE FONDANT
125g quality dark chocolate
130g unsalted butter
25g plain flour
2 large free range eggs
3 egg yolks
50g caster sugar

FOR THE MASCARPONE
200g mascarpone
45g icing sugar
1/2 vanilla pod, seeds from the pod
50g hazelnuts, roasted, peeled and chopped
50g quality white chocolate, melted

METHOD:

Place the chocolate and butter into a metal bowl and melt over a pan of boiling water. Whilst the chocolate is melting, place eggs and sugar into a food mixer with a whisk attachment and whisk on high speed until the mixture has become twice its volume and white in colour, make sure to keep your eye on the chocolate when the eggs are whisking as you don't want to burn the chocolate! Now, with the egg mixture still whisking but, now at a slow speed add the melted chocolate and butter onto the eggs until it is completely mixed together. Take the mix from the machine and fold in the flour. And finally, the trickiest part of the recipe, you will need 4 1/2 pint disposable tin foil dishes or as a chef would use, a dariol mould. Butter these dishes and divide the mix evenly between them and refrigerate them for 1/2 hour and then bake in a pre-heated oven of 200°C for 12 minutes. Take out of the oven and turn out onto a plate and voilà the proof is in the pudding!

Now, the mascarpone is fairly simple, place the cheese into a metal bowl and fold in the vanilla and sugar until they are well mixed together, then, with the melted white chocolate the trick is to make sure the white chocolate is not too hot as this will split when added to the mascarpone. Once this is added all you have to do is fold in the chopped hazelnuts and allow to cool and then serve.

The only other item that you will ever need with this dish is fresh raspberries.

Malcolm Goble
Head Chef

THE SAMLING, WINDERMERE

Ambleside Road, Windermere, Cumbria, LA23 1LR. Telephone: 01539 431922

LANGOUSTINES WITH AVOCADO CROQUETTE AND LIME JELLY

SERVES: 4
PREPARATION TIME: 30 MINUTES
FREEZER TIME: 30 MINUTES

INGREDIENTS:
1 kilo langoustines
INGREDIENTS FOR CROQUETTE
1 ripe avocado
2 vine tomatoes peeled and diced
Tabasco
100g breadcrumbs
1 beaten egg
Juice of 1 lemon
LIME JELLY
Half lemon
2 limes
Half red chilli
200ml water
25g sugar
2 leaves gelatine

METHOD:
Peel avocado and cut half into small dice, with the rest crush with a fork and mix with the tomato, diced avocado, lemon juice, tabasco to taste, salt and pepper. Shape with two spoons to a cylinder, place on a tray and freeze for 30 minutes, when firm dip into beaten egg and then the breadcrumbs.

LIME JELLY
Grate lime zest, then juice the lemon and limes, add the chilli, sugar and water, boil for 10 minutes and pass through a fine sieve, simmer to a light syrup, soak the gelatine and add to the syrup, set in an ice cube tray.

TO ASSEMBLE
Deep fry the croquette at 170°C until golden brown, keep warm in a low oven, turn out a jelly and place onto a plate, in a hot non-stick pan add a little olive oil and then the langoustines, fry for 2 minutes. Season and put on kitchen paper to drain, place the langoustines next to the jelly and the croquette.

Nigel Mendham
Head Chef

CHEF SAYS...

NIGEL MENDHAM IS THE HEAD CHEF FOR THE SAMLING

“ The lime jelly is best prepared a day in advance, allowing time to set, a good garnish for the dish is wild rocket dressed in olive oil and greek yoghurt. ”

Nigel Mendham

CHEF SAYS...

PETER W. TEAGUE IS THE HEAD CHEF FOR THE TUDOR FARMHOUSE

> " The beautiful Forest of Dean is a hidden treasure that is easily accessible. Like the Forest, this pudding is a treasure trove that delights the senses. "

Peter W. Teague

DATE & BANANA PUDDING WITH TOFFEE SAUCE

SERVES: 6

INGREDIENTS:
PUDDING
4oz soft butter
12oz dark brown sugar
2 ripe bananas
1lb plain flour
2 tablespoons baking powder
2 eggs, beaten
12oz chopped dates
1 pint boiling water
2 teaspoons bicarbonate of soda
TOFFEE SAUCE
3oz butter
5oz dark brown sugar
4floz double cream

METHOD:
Pre-heat oven to 170°C/Gas Mark 3. Grease and dust with flour 8″ square cake tin. Cream butter and sugar in a mixer until smooth and fluffy.

Mash bananas with fork and add to butter and sugar. Measure boiling water into a large container, add dates to soften and mix in bicarbonate of soda. Sift flour and baking powder together, beat eggs. Add flour and eggs to banana mixture a little at a time, beating all the time.

Add dates to the above mixture beating slowly. Once fully incorporated pour into prepared cake tin, cook for approximately 40-45 minutes until firm to the touch.

TO MAKE TOFFEE SAUCE
Place all ingredients in thick bottomed saucepan. Stir until all are combined. Simmer for 5 minutes stirring occasionally. (Sauce should be slightly thickened and glossy.)

Remove cake from oven. Serve warm, glazed with toffee sauce and vanilla ice-cream. Enjoy!

Peter W. Teague
Head Chef

CHEF SAYS...

FRANCES ATKINS IS THE HEAD CHEF FOR THE YORKE ARMS

" When roasting the butternut squash, put a little water in with the olive oil to achieve good caramelisation. This dish can be used as a vegetarian dish, using raisins instead of mutton. "

Frances Atkins

MUTTON, HORSERADISH LENTILS, SQUASH, BEETROOT RELISH

INGREDIENTS:

2 shanks of mutton
Selection of vegetables (swede is especially good with mutton)
Herbs, parsley, oregano and fennel
Small bottle of cider, with 1/2 pt vegetable stock
4 small shallots
3oz cream
FOR THE BEETROOT RELISH
450g beetroot peeled and grated (coarsely)
225g onion, chopped
3 tablespoons sugar
1floz (25ml) white wine vinegar
4floz (120ml) red wine
2 juniper berries
Salt and freshly ground pepper
FOR THE LENTILS AND SQUASH
250g lentil du puy
1 shallot
1 carrot
1 bunch thyme
1 stick grated horseradish
1 butternut squash
Sea salt
Black pepper
White wine
FOR THE CARAMELISED APPLES
Cooking apples, sugar and cloves

METHOD:

TO PREPARE MUTTON

Brown mutton shanks in hot sauté pan with vegetables and herbs, transfer to oven and cover with stock and cider. Braise shank in a slow oven, cook for approximately 2 hours at 180°C. When cooked the meat should fall off the shank, when removed from the liquid. Strain and discard the vegetables, skim off fat, reduce the liquid until halved.

Place meat in the reduced liquid with small shallots and finish with a touch of cream.

BEETROOT RELISH

Sweat the onions slowly in olive oil until very soft. Add sugar and seasoning and allow to brown slightly. Add all other ingredients and cook gently for 30 minutes.

LENTILS AND SQUASH

Wash lentils and cook with white wine, finely chopped shallot, carrot and thyme. Peel and de-seed the butternut squash, cut in half,

roast in olive oil at 200°C until lightly browned and cooked (15 minutes approximately). Remove from oven and slice on the cross. Stir horseradish into cooked lentils, season and spoon alongside squash.

CARAMELISE APPLES

Peel and slice apples and poach in a little sugar and water. Caramelise in a pan with sugar and cloves.

TO SERVE

Serve the mutton in a bowl with caramelised apple on top alongside lentils, beetroot relish and roast squash.

Frances Atkins
Head Chef

CITRUS PANNACOTTA WITH BASIL ICE CREAM

INGREDIENTS:

CITRUS PANNACOTTA
125ml Guernsey full cream milk
125ml Guernsey whipping cream
25g caster sugar
1 vanilla pod, split lengthways
75g mascarpone cheese
1 tablespoon marsala, 1.25 leaves gelatine
Finely grated zest of 1/2 lime, lemon & orange

BASIL ICE CREAM
100ml Guernsey full cream milk
200ml Guernsey whipping cream
25g caster sugar
4 egg yolks
150g white chocolate, finely chopped
1 packet fresh basil
(Guernsey whipping cream has a high fat content
and can be substituted with double cream.)

BUTTER BISCUITS
2 egg whites, 60g unsalted butter, melted
40g plain flour, sieved, 50g icing sugar, sieved

METHOD:

CITRUS PANNACOTTA

Place the leaf gelatine into a small bowl with the marsala, leave to soften for several minutes. Bring to boiling point the cream & milk with sugar, zest of citrus fruits and split vanilla pod. Remove from heat and discard the vanilla pod ensuring all those flavoursome seeds have been scraped from within. Place the marsala and gelatine over the hot saucepan until the gelatine has dissolved, pour into the hot cream.

Whisk the mascarpone into the hot cream mixture and pour through a fine sieve. Allow cooling before pouring into your chosen moulds. This can be done a day in advance as the pannacotta requires several hours to set. To serve dip each mould into a dish of hot water briefly before turning the pannacotta out.

BASIL ICE CREAM

Pick the basil leaves and place the stalks into a thick bottomed saucepan with the milk and cream, bring to scalding point, add the finely chopped chocolate and allow to infuse for several minutes. Meanwhile whisk together the caster sugar and egg yolks until light in colour. Sieve the heated milk, cream and chocolate mixture onto this and cook gently on a low heat, stirring continuously to prevent the mixture scrambling. Remove from heat and allow to cool. When cool add the picked basil leaves and place in kitchen blender and blitz the liquid briefly to incorporate the basil leaves. Place the liquid into an ice cream machine and proceed to freeze. Alternatively place directly into your freezer in a sealed container and stir the mixture at regular intervals, though this won't produce the same smooth creaminess. The ice cream can also be prepared a day or two in advance.

Tony Leck
Owner/Chef

CHEF SAYS...

TONY LECK IS OWNER/CHEF OF THE PAVILION

" I like to serve it with a few seasonal strawberries splashed with a little aged balsamic vinegar and freshly ground black peppercorns! "

Tony Leck

CHEF SAYS...

STEPHEN WHEELER IS EXECUTIVE CHEF FOR DELAWARE NORTH COMPANIES AT WEMBLEY STADIUM

Stephen Wheeler

" My philosophy on food is all about quality produce, prepared simply, being unfussy and unpretentious, letting the food speak for itself, with emphasis on flavour and taste. "

PAVÉ OF SEA BASS, ROAST FENNEL, BABY SQUASH, LEMON & PARSLEY DRESSING

INGREDIENTS:
150g sea bass, scaled & pin boned
30g fennel
15g green baby squash
15g yellow baby squash
5ml olive oil
5g garlic
1 thyme sprig
40g ratte potato
2g salt & pepper
10ml lemon oil & parsley dressing

METHOD:

SEA BASS PREPARATION

Score sea bass five times. Season and sear skin side down in hot pan until lightly coloured, turn sea bass and cook for further 2-3 minutes.

VEGETABLE PREPARATION

Cook ratte potatoes in boiling salted water until tender, drain and allow to cool. Quarter baby squash and dice fennel to same size. Crush garlic, add thyme, olive oil, baby squash and fennel.

Roast in oven until coloured, once cooked squeeze with lemon, allow to cool. Cut ratte potatoes into 6 wedges, season and coat with olive oil mix from baby squash and fennel. Roast in oven until golden brown.

DRESSING PREPARATION

Chop flat leaf parsley, add lemon zest and blitz with extra virgin olive oil.

SERVICE

Mix potatoes, fennel and baby squash, adjust seasoning. Arrange on plate and place sea bass on top in centre of vegetables. Drizzle dressing as shown in photo.

Stephen Wheeler
Executive Chef

WESTBEACH, BOURNEMOUTH

Pier Approach, Bournemouth. Telephone: 01202 587785 Online: www.west-beach.co.uk

CHEF SAYS...

GREG ETHERIDGE IS HEAD CHEF AT WESTBEACH RESTAURANT

> "Tuna is a lovely meaty fish which stands up well to the strong flavour of horseradish, grating it fresh into the mash at the last minute will give a nice kick to your dish."

Greg Etheridge

SEARED LOIN OF TUNA, HORSERADISH MASH AND SAUTÉED WILD MUSHROOMS

SERVES: 4
PREPARATION TIME: 20 MINUTES
COOKING TIME: 30 MINUTES

INGREDIENTS:

4 x 200g tuna steaks
500g Maris Piper or Desirée potatoes, peeled and diced
200g unsalted butter
20ml milk
10ml double cream
4 tablespoons creamed horseradish
8g fresh horseradish
Salt, white pepper
400g mixed wild mushrooms, cleaned
1 small shallot, diced
2 tablespoons olive oil
120g wild roquette
Balsamic vinegar
Olive oil

METHOD:

Place the potatoes in a large pan, cover with cold water, add salt and bring to the boil. Reduce the heat and simmer for 20 minutes or until the potato will break under a little pressure. Drain well and return to the pan drying any excess moisture out over a very low heat. Warm the butter with the milk and cream and mash into the potatoes. (For a more refined mash, a potato ricer may be used before you add the warm liquid). Add the creamed and grated horseradish and check for taste.

In a small pan add the diced shallot and sweat with no colour, add the mushrooms and fry over a high heat, season to taste.

Lightly oil and season the tuna steaks. Heat a non-stick pan on a high heat and carefully lay the steaks down on one side.

After 2 minutes turn the fish over and cook for another 2 minutes, this should give a rare-medium piece of fish. If you prefer your tuna more well cooked simply turn the heat down a little and add an extra 3-4 minutes to the cooking time.

Lightly dress the roquette with olive oil. To finish drizzle olive oil and balsamic vinegar around the dish.

Greg Etheridge
Head Chef

CHEF SAYS...

MARTIN BURGE IS THE HEAD CHEF FOR THE WHATLEY MANOR

" We often over whip the egg whites... chefs make this mistake all the time, so don't be frightened to start again. Correcting this is the key to making a successful soufflé. "

Martin Burge

BANANA SOUFFLÉ

INGREDIENTS:
PASTRY CREAM
1 egg yolk
23g sugar
90 ml milk
5g cornflour
2 drops of banana essence
BANANA PURÉE
62g of peeled banana
Pinch of sugar
20g of butter
BANANA SOUFFLE
90g of pastry cream
Six egg whites
15g of sugar

METHOD:
PASTRY CREAM
Boil in a saucepan 90ml of milk. In a mixing bowl mix 1 egg yolk, 18g of sugar, 5g of cornflour, 5g of plain flour. Add the boiling milk into the mix, return to a medium heat and continue to stir for 2 minutes. Take off heat and allow to cool before use.

BANANA PURÉE
Lay the bananas on greaseproof paper. Brush with melted butter. Sprinkle with sugar. Place into a pre-heated oven, Gas Mark 6/200°C/400°F. Remove from oven once banana has caramelised

BANANA SOUFFLÉ
In a large bowl whisk the pastry cream and banana purée to form a smooth paste. Whisk the egg whites with sugar to form smooth firm peak. Fold egg whites into the banana mixture (do not over mix). Pour the mixture into buttered ramekins and cook in a pre-heated oven, Gas Mark 5/180°C/360°F for approximately 9-10 minutes.

Martin Burge
Head Chef

FILLETS OF LEMON SOLE WITH SALMON SLAW AND MARSH SAMPHIRE

SERVES: 2-4
PREPARATION TIME: 30 MINUTES
COOKING TIME: 10 MINUTES

INGREDIENTS:
8 lemon sole fillets
1 small celeriac, peeled and grated
10 slices smoked salmon, sliced julienne
1 shallot, finely sliced
Seasoning
Parsley, chopped
Mayonnaise to bind
500g samphire
SAUCE
1 shallot, finely sliced
1 glass white wine
150g butter, unsalted
20ml double cream
2 lemons, juiced
Seasoning

METHOD:
Peel and grate celeriac and lightly season. Add chopped parsley, smoked salmon and sliced shallot and mix well with mayonnaise in a large bowl. Taste and season.

Place lemon sole fillets onto a buttered baking tray, season and cook under preheated grill for 5-7 minutes. Cut off roots from samphire and wash well. Bring to boil in fresh boiling water and cook until tender - a few minutes. Place in warm dish and add a knob of butter.

SAUCE
Sweat shallot in butter until soft, add wine and reduce by half. Add cream and reduce by half again. Take off heat and whisk in butter and add the lemon juice.

TO SERVE
Arrange samphire in middle of dish with lemon sole fillets on top. Pour over lemon butter sauce. Add a generous spoonful of salmon slaw to the dish and serve with new potatoes.

Nicholas Parker
Head Chef

Nicholas Parker

CHEF SAYS...
NICHOLAS PARKER IS THE HEAD CHEF FOR THE WHITE HORSE

" If you are unable to obtain samphire - a fleshy succulent, smooth and much branched herb that grows on coastal marshland - substitute with baby asparagus or young spinach. "

136

WINTERINGHAM FIELDS, WINTERINGHAM

North Lincolnshire, DN15 9PF. Telephone: 01724 733096 Email: Wintfields@aol.com Online: www.winteringhamfields.com

CHEF SAYS...

ROBERT THOMPSON IS THE HEAD CHEF FOR WINTERINGHAM FIELDS

" How can you ever stop learning about food? How can you say you have reached the top? That is somewhere I would like to get, where I could say that I am satisfied, but is there such a place? "

Robert Thompson

SEARED SCOTTISH SCALLOPS WITH PIGS TROTTER, CÈPES & THEIR OWN SAUCES

SERVES: TWO AS A STARTER

INGREDIENTS:

1 pig's trotter, boned out down to first joint
80g minced pork
20g foie gras
30g ham hock, braised until soft in court bouillon
1 egg
5g sage, chopped
5g thyme, chopped
4 scallops in shell
60g scallop roe
200g cèpes
300ml chicken stock
300ml light red wine
500ml pork stock
1 clove garlic
50g brown sugar
100ml white wine
50g mixed salad leaves: mizuno, chard, tatsoi and frisée
100ml cream
200ml scallop stock
2 medium shallots, finely chopped

METHOD:

Bring to simmer the pork stock. Place the trotter skin into the stock and cook very slowly until the skin is soft. Blend the pork mince with the egg, foie gras, sage, thyme and seasoning then fold in the ham hock and mix well, check seasoning by poaching a small amount wrapped in cling film. Taste then re-season if necessary. Trim the trotter skin and fill with the farce, roll up lightly in foil and poach in the pork stock for a further 20 minutes.

Prepare the scallops and set aside the meat. Blanch the scallop roes, slice in half and rinse out well. Sauté the finely chopped shallot add the scallop roes and white wine then the scallop stock, bring to simmer and reduce by half, add 50ml of cream and blitz until smooth. Pass through a fine sieve.

For the cèpe sauce, sauté the remaining shallot, add the trimmings from all the cèpes as well as half the original quantity. Add the chicken stock, thyme stalks and garlic.

Reduce until cèpes are soft, blitz and pass through a fine sieve then add the rest of the cream. Check seasoning.

Reduce the red wine and brown sugar until syrupy then allow to cool.
Reduce the pork stock used to cook trotter until sauce consistency. Finish with butter. Sauté the remaining cèpes and season well. Slice the pig's trotter and seal in pan adding a wine reduction to coat base of each roundels.

Sear the scallops and then dress. Start with the scallop roe, cèpes sauce, pig's trotter and the scallops. Dress the salad leaves and arrange evenly. As a garnish, place celery fritter, ham hock fritter and pancetta crisps around the plate.

Robert Thompson
Head Chef

137

CHEF SAYS...
ANTONY WORRALL THOMPSON

" I'm pleased to be able to contribute to this special book, 'This is my Favourite', and I hope YOU will make it one of YOUR favourite cookbooks too. It's for a great cause. "

Antony Worrall Thompson

SEARED SOY-GLAZED TUNA LOIN, ASIAN CRUNCH SALAD

SERVES: 4

INGREDIENTS:
1 tablespoon jasmine rice, uncooked
2 dried red chillies
500g (1lb 2oz) tuna loin
2 tablespoons sesame oil
75ml (2½ floz) kecap manis (sweet soy sauce)
2 teaspoons sugar
4 tablespoons lime juice
3 tablespoons Thai fish sauce
1 small cucumber, peeled, halved lengthways, de-seeded, and cut into 1cm (½ inch) slices
2 red shallots, finely sliced
12 cherry tomatoes, halved
2 red chillies, finely sliced
1 handful fresh mint leaves, roughly chopped
1 handful fresh coriander leaves
2 tablespoons fresh basil leaves, ripped
4 spring onions, finely sliced

METHOD:

Heat a dry frying pan, add the rice and chillies and toast until golden but not burnt. Grind the mix in a clean coffee grinder or pound to a powder and set aside.

Chargrill or pan-fry the tuna all over for around 2 minutes, until well marked outside and rare inside. Place in a bowl and leave to rest for 10 minutes. Meanwhile, combine the sesame oil with the kecap manis and pour over the fillet. Marinate for 2 hours, turning from time to time.

Meanwhile, dissolve the sugar in the lime juice and fish sauce. Combine the cucumber, shallots, cherry tomatoes, red chillies, herbs and spring onions in a large bowl. Add the lime juice and fish sauce mixture and toss to combine.

Slice the tuna thinly. Toss some of the ground rice mix through the salad with any cooking juices that have collected in the bowl. Pile high on a large plate and arrange the tuna around the salad. Brush the tuna with the marinade just before serving.

At Notting Grill we believe in buying the best ingredients and treating them simply. No fuss, no frills.

Antony Worrall Thompson

Antony Worrall Thompson

CRISP VEAL SWEETBREAD SPRING ROLL ON SCALLION AND MANGE TOUT SALAD

SERVES: 10

INGREDIENTS:

FOR THE SPRING ROLLS
3 litre of vegetable oil
1.5kg veal sweetbreads
1 packet spring roll pastry
100g ginger, 2 green chillies, 2 red chillies
1 egg

FOR THE SALAD
500g mange tout, 1 shallot
1 bunch spring onion, 2 heads curly endive
1 bunch of coriander, 2 limes
200g pink ginger
1 cucumber

FOR THE DRESSING
50g palm sugar
20ml of rice wine vinegar
40ml chicken stock
2 limes

METHOD:

DRESSING
In a saucepan gently heat up the palm sugar with two tablespoons of stock until it dissolves. Turn up the heat and caramelize the sugar until golden brown (this burns very easily).

Now add the vinegar and bring back to the boil, add the chicken stock and over low heat reduce to thick syrup. Drain and leave to cool. When cold press in the juice of two limes and season with salt and pepper. This will keep for up to four days in the fridge.

SALAD
Cut the scallions, shallot and the mange tout in fine julienne. Clean and wash the curly endive only keeping the nice yellow tips in the middle. Slice the cucumber very thinly.

SPRING ROLL
Thoroughly wash the sweetbreads under cold water. In salted boiling water blanch the sweetbreads for about five minutes, refresh in ice water and place on a dry cloth.

Now peel off all the fat and the skin that can be seen on the sweetbreads, after doing that cut into one inch cubes. Peel and then grate the ginger, cut the chillies in half remove the seeds and chop into small dices.

Heat up a large pan with some vegetable oil, place the sweetbreads, ginger and chillies into the pan and slightly brown all over. The mixture should be still fairly raw in the middle. Remove from the pan onto a dry cloth and leave to cool. Season with salt and pepper.

Place one sheet of spring roll pastry onto a chopping board and brush with egg all over, place another sheet on top of the first one so you get a thicker sheet. Place two tablespoons of the mixture onto the bottom of the pastry, fold in the ends and roll up.

Heat up the oil to 175°F. Fry the spring rolls in the oil until golden brown, take out and leave to cool down for one minute. Assemble as per picture.

Peter Wallner
Head Chef

Peter Wallner

ZAIKA, LONDON

No.1 Kensington High Street, London, W8 5NP. Telephone: 020 7795 6533

CHEF SAYS...

SANJAY DWIVEDI IS THE HEAD CHEF FOR ZAIKA

" I spent 6 months in the Maldives, the local fisherman brought me a sailfish which I cooked with the recipe below. It's not so easy to get sailfish in the UK but to remind me of that time, I use fresh Tuna instead. "

Sanjay Dwivedi

BLUE FIN TUNA DUSTED WITH SPICES, WITH CRAB 'DOKHLA' & INDIAN CAVIAR

INGREDIENTS:

SPICES FOR TUNA
3 teaspoons whole coriander seeds
3 teaspoons whole fennel seeds
1½ teaspoons whole green cardamom
2 dried whole red chillies

CRAB 'DOKHLA'
70g polenta
10g chickpea flour
½ teaspoon baking powder
Pinch of salt
60g double cream
75g brown crabmeat
30g white crabmeat
2 chilli chopped, 1 red pepper, chopped
2 eggs

TEMPERING AND COOKING OF THE CRAB 'DOKHLA'
2 teaspoons mustard seeds
6 teaspoons olive oil
6 curry leaves
20g grated coconut

CRAB CHUTNEY
50g white crab meat
60g thick yoghurt
1 red chilli chopped
2 sprigs chopped coriander
½ lemon juice

INDIAN CAVIAR
2 teaspoons mustard seeds, 4 teaspoons olive oil

METHOD:

SPICES FOR TUNA
Blitz ingredients coarsely in a grinder and keep in airtight container. Can be done 3 days prior.

CRAB 'DOKHLA'
Sieve polenta, chickpea flour, baking powder and salt into a mixing bowl. Mix rest of the ingredients well and slowly add to above. Leave in fridge for 20 minutes.

TEMPERING AND COOKING OF THE 'DOKHLA'
Add oil to a hot pan, splatter mustard seeds until they pop, add curry leaf, coconut and sauté for couple of minutes. Add this to the crab 'dokhla' mix. Grease ¼ inch tray with olive oil, place the above mix, flatten and cook in the oven at 170°C for 20-30 minutes. Once cold enough to handle cut into 6cm x 6cm, keep aside. The 'dokhla' can be made up to 3 days in advance.

CRAB CHUTNEY
Mix all and check for seasoning. Keep aside in the fridge.

INDIAN CAVIAR
Heat oil in a pan, splatter mustard seeds until they pop and crackle.

ASSEMBLY
Dust tuna with spices. Heat pan, add a couple of teaspoons of olive oil and cook tuna very quickly ensuring not to overcook it. Warm up the 'dokhla' in oven, place at the bottom of the plate, the tuna goes on top, place the coconut chutney on next to it. Garnish with a small amount of mustard seeds. Serve with salad greens.

Sanjay Dwivedi
Head Chef

YANG SING, MANCHESTER

34 Princess Street, Manchester, M1 4JY. Telephone: 0161 236 2200 Facsimile: 0161 236 5934 Email: info@yang-sing.com Online: www.yang-sing.com

CHEF SAYS...

HARRY YEUNG IS THE EXECUTIVE CHEF AND OWNER OF YANG SING

" It was an honour to be asked to contribute to such a worthwhile cause as BBC Children in Need. Children have always been very important and special visitors at Yang Sing. "

Harry Yeung

LEMON AND HONEY SESAME SEED PRAWNS

SERVES: 4-6

INGREDIENTS:

FOR THE SAUCE
8 floz water
Pinch salt
2 teaspoons clear honey
1 quarter of a fresh lemon, sliced
2oz sugar
2 floz Robinson's whole lemon drink
2 floz white vinegar
2oz custard powder

FOR THE PRAWNS
1/2 lb prawns, with shells on
1 egg beaten and ready to use
1 teaspoon potato or corn starch mixed with
1 teaspoon water
1 pinch of salt
1 pinch of white pepper
1/2 lb of sesame seeds, spread
onto a large plate
1/2 pint vegetable oil
Two leaves of iceberg lettuce, shredded and placed
on serving dish

METHOD:

PRAWNS

Peel shells off prawns leaving the tail intact. Cut the prawn down the middle up to the tail and fan out to form a butterfly shape. Clean and rinse then dry with paper towel. Add salt, white pepper and wet potato/corn starch to prawns. Add egg and mix well. Place prawns onto sesame seeds and turn over, so that both sides are evenly coated in seeds. Heat vegetable oil in wok or deep pan to 190°C. Cook prawns for 4 minutes in hot oil. Lift prawns out, drain off excess oil and place onto serving dish on top of shredded lettuce.

SAUCE

Place the ingredients for the sauce (except vinegar and custard powder) into a pan, bring to the boil then add the vinegar.

Thicken with the custard powder, until it reaches the consistency of evaporated milk, pour over prawns.

Harry Yeung
Executive Chef and Owner